Domestic vs. Offshore Manufacturing

Other Books in the Current Controversies Series

Domestic vs. Offshore Manufacturing

Sabine Cherenfant, Book Editor

GREENHAVEN
PUBLISHING

Published in 2022 by Greenhaven Publishing, LLC
353 3rd Avenue, Suite 255, New York, NY 10010

First Edition

Articles in Greenhaven Publishing anthologies are often edited for length to meet page
requirements. In addition, original titles of these works are changed to clearly present
the main thesis and to explicitly indicate the author's opinion. Every effort is made to
ensure that Greenhaven Publishing accurately reflects the original intent of the authors.
Every effort has been made to trace the owners of the copyrighted material.

Cover image: anucha sirivisansuwan/Getty Images

Library of Congress Cataloging-in-Publication Data

Names: Cherenfant, Sabine, editor.
Title: Domestic vs. offshore manufacturing / Sabine Cherenfant, book
    editor.
Other titles: Domestic versus offshore manufacturing
Description: First edition. | New York : Greenhaven Publishing, 2022. |
    Series: Current controversies | Includes bibliographical references and
    index. | Audience: Grades 9–12.
Identifiers: LCCN 2020004608 | ISBN 9781534507128 (library binding) | ISBN
    9781534507111 (paperback) | ISBN 9781534507135 (ebook)
Subjects: LCSH: Offshore assembly industry—Juvenile literature. |
    Manufacturing industries—Juvenile literature.
Classification: LCC HD9720.5 .D66 2022 | DDC 338.4/767042—dc23
LC record available at https://lccn.loc.gov/2020004608

Manufactured in the United States of America

Website: http://greenhavenpublishing.com

Contents

Chapter 1: Does Offshore Manufacturing Benefit Companies?

Kimberly Amadeo

Though outsourcing does impact the domestic job market, the case for manufacturing abroad vs. domestically proves to be a complex debate. Companies that outsource are faced with the need to compete globally and cut costs, but there is also the colossal need to support the domestic labor market.

Yes: Offshoring Helps Companies Stay Afloat

Diversify OSS

There are five important reasons why companies turn to offshore manufacturing: lower cost, restrictive domestic regulations, the need to compete, higher quality goods, and domestic skill shortage. Offshoring helps companies tackle those issues and allows them to stay competitive in the domestic and global markets.

Nathan Resnick

By offshoring production to China, companies are not only significantly cutting costs, but they are also widening their market reach and expanding their production capacity. Counterfeit products are indeed an issue, but working with sourcing platforms helps prevent this.

Theo Anderson

Alone, the low cost of labor overseas is not enough of a reason for a company to outsource production—the price of transportation and other hidden costs are important factors as well. This viewpoint explains a model developed by Jan Van Mieghem and Robert Boute to help companies determine if domestic manufacturing would cost them less than offshore manufacturing. For many companies, offshoring proves to be vital for survival.

No: Offshoring Costs Companies More in the Long Run and Affects Domestic Wages

Adam Hersh and Ethan Gurwitz

Globalization puts a lot of pressure on local job markets because production tends to be moved to foreign countries with lower labor costs. This means that offshoring plays a significant role in driving domestic wages downward.

Global Manufacturing Services, Inc.

Before moving production abroad, companies must take into consideration the hidden costs associated with offshoring. Even though offshore manufacturing helps companies keep labor costs down, hidden expenses make up an additional 27 percent in costs accrued.

Robert Handfield

Product recalls are not often addressed in discussions about offshore manufacturing. Nevertheless, in addition to product delays and distribution issues, quality defects are a relatively common problem that results in recalls and additional costs to businesses.

Chapter 2: Does Offshore Manufacturing Help the Economies of Developing Countries?

Rice University

When offshoring, companies need to first understand the local culture of the community with which they intend to work. Moreover, as companies globalize and become increasingly interconnected, they will need to heed local ethical considerations as well.

Yes: Offshoring Helps Developing Countries Fight Extreme Poverty and Raise Their GDP

No: Offshore Manufacturing Is Unethical and Does Not Benefit Hosting Countries

Even though offshoring is often blamed as a major cause of domestic job loss, Schultze explains in this viewpoint that US unemployment can be more accurately blamed on productivity acceleration than offshored jobs, at least as of 2003. Moreover, when companies are able to produce items at a cheaper rate, it helps improve domestic wages and living standards.

No: Offshore Manufacturing Causes Job Loss and Negatively Impacts Standards of Living

the price abroad. This helps foreign workers but jeopardizes the American workforce.

Chapter 4: Is Domestic Manufacturing Less Harmful to the Environment?

production. As a result, those hosting countries are now paying the environmental price for it.

K. S. Venkatachalam

More than 4.2 million deaths globally are attributed to air pollution. Factors like overpopulation and vehicle exhaust contribute to toxic air pollution in India and China, but air pollution is also a result of industrialization and manufacturing practices in those countries.

No: Environmental Concerns Affect All Countries, Regardless of Where Manufacturing Occurs

Nate Berg

The most polluted city in the United States is Bakersfield, California. Oil refinement is one of the main causes of the poor air quality, and although efforts are being made to curb the issue, this shows that environmental concerns caused by industrialization are present in all countries, despite stricter regulations in the United States.

US Energy Information Administration

Data on the United States' energy production and consumption helps to illustrate the environmental impact that practices like drilling have on the climate. Efforts to minimize environmental impact are not always effective.

Foreword

Controversy" is a word that has an undeniably unpleasant connotation. It carries a definite negative charge. Controversy can spoil family gatherings, spread a chill around classroom and campus discussion, inflame public discourse, open raw civic wounds, and lead to the ouster of public officials. We often feel that controversy is almost akin to bad manners, a rude and shocking eruption of that which must not be spoken or thought of in polite, tightly guarded society. To avoid controversy, to quell controversy, is often seen as a public good, a victory for etiquette, perhaps even a moral or ethical imperative.

Yet the studious, deliberate avoidance of controversy is also a whitewashing, a denial, a death threat to democracy. It is a false sterilizing and sanitizing and superficial ordering of the messy, ragged, chaotic, at times ugly processes by which a healthy democracy identifies and confronts challenges, engages in passionate debate about appropriate approaches and solutions, and arrives at something like a consensus and a broadly accepted and supported way forward. Controversy is the megaphone, the speaker's corner, the public square through which the citizenry finds and uses its voice. Controversy is the life's blood of our democracy and absolutely essential to the vibrant health of our society.

Our present age is certainly no stranger to controversy. We are consumed by fierce debates about technology, privacy, political correctness, poverty, violence, crime and policing, guns, immigration, civil and human rights, terrorism, militarism, environmental protection, and gender and racial equality. Loudly competing voices are raised every day, shouting opposing opinions, putting forth competing agendas, and summoning starkly different visions of a utopian or dystopian future. Often these voices attempt to shout the others down; there is precious little listening and considering among the cacophonous din. Yet listening and considering, too, are essential to the health of a democracy. If controversy is democracy's lusty lifeblood, respectful listening and careful thought are its higher faculties, its brain, its conscience.

Current Controversies does not shy away from or attempt to hush the loudly competing voices. It seeks to provide readers with as wide and representative as possible a range of articulate voices on any given controversy of the day, separates each one out to allow it to be heard clearly and fairly, and encourages careful listening to each of these well-crafted, thoughtfully expressed opinions, supplied by some of today's leading academics, thinkers, analysts, politicians, policy makers, economists, activists, change agents, and advocates. Only after listening to a wide range of opinions on an issue, evaluating the strengths and weaknesses of each argument, assessing how well the facts and available evidence mesh with the stated opinions and conclusions, and thoughtfully and critically examining one's own beliefs and conscience can the reader begin to arrive at his or her own conclusions and articulate his or her own stance on the spotlighted controversy.

This process is facilitated and supported in each Current Controversies volume by an introduction and chapter overviews that provide readers with the essential context they need to begin engaging with the spotlighted controversies, with the debates surrounding them, and with their own perhaps shifting or nascent opinions on them. Chapters are organized around several key questions that are answered with diverse opinions representing all points on the political spectrum. In its content, organization, and methodology, readers are encouraged to determine the authors' point of view and purpose, interrogate and analyze the various arguments and their rhetoric and structure, evaluate the arguments' strengths and weaknesses, test their claims against available facts and evidence, judge the validity of the reasoning, and bring into clearer, sharper focus the reader's own beliefs and conclusions and how they may differ from or align with those in the collection or those of classmates.

Research has shown that reading comprehension skills improve dramatically when students are provided with compelling, intriguing, and relevant "discussable" texts. The subject matter of these collections could not be more compelling, intriguing, or urgently relevant to today's students and the world they are poised to inherit. The anthologized articles also provide the basis for stimulating, lively, and passionate classroom debates. Students who are compelled to anticipate objections to their own argument and identify the flaws in those of an opponent read more carefully, think more critically, and steep themselves in relevant context, facts, and information more thoroughly. In short, using discussable text of the kind provided by every single volume in the Current Controversies series encourages close reading, facilitates reading comprehension, fosters research, strengthens critical thinking, and greatly enlivens and energizes classroom discussion and participation. The entire learning process is deepened, extended, and strengthened.

If we are to foster a knowledgeable, responsible, active, and engaged citizenry, we must provide readers with the intellectual, interpretive, and critical-thinking tools and experience necessary to make sense of the world around them and of the all-important debates and arguments that inform it. We must encourage them not to run away from or attempt to quell controversy but to embrace it in a responsible, conscientious, and thoughtful way, to sharpen and strengthen their own informed opinions by listening to and critically analyzing those of others. This series encourages respectful engagement with and analysis of current controversies and competing opinions and fosters a resulting increase in the strength and rigor of one's own opinions and stances. As such, it helps readers assume their rightful place in the public square and provides them with the skills necessary to uphold their awesome responsibility—guaranteeing the continued and future health of a vital, vibrant, and free democracy.

Introduction

> *"Outsourcing is inevitable, and I don't think it's necessarily treating people like things."*
>
> *-Stephen Covey, American educator, author, and businessman*

Offshore manufacturing is not a new concept. In fact, according to the *Encyclopedia Britannica*, offshoring is a practice that blossomed in the mid-twentieth century.[1] It is mostly an alternative production option intended to help companies lower the cost of production and maximize profit. The *Encyclopedia Britannica* also outlines the main reasons for offshoring, which include access to a cheaper workforce, weaker environmental and labor laws in developing countries, better tax alternatives, and quick access to "raw materials."[1] The debate over domestic vs. offshore manufacturing has permeated presidential debates and raised numerous arguments over whether or not offshore manufacturing benefits both the hosting countries and home countries. There are various substantial arguments for and against offshoring, with three particular aspects that are worth considering: its positive and negative domestic outcomes, its outcomes for hosting countries, and its impact on the environment.

As previously stated, one of the main reasons why companies are pushed to offshore some or all of their operations is because of the financial benefits. As highlighted by the US Department of Commerce, the cost of labor in the United States is considerably higher than the cost in other countries.[2] Bonnie Kavoussi of *HuffPost* writes that Chinese factory workers, on average, only make 10 percent of what their American counterparts earn in hourly wages.[3] Yet the US Department of Commerce points out that companies cannot solely rely on hourly wages to determine whether or not it would be beneficial for them to move operations abroad. For instance, quick turnarounds, rising minimum wages in other countries, and the complications of exchange rates are all variables that will affect overseas costs and might make offshore manufacturing more costly than domestic manufacturing in the long run.[4]

One of the primary concerns and controversies around offshore manufacturing is its potential effect on the domestic job market. If jobs are being moved abroad, what does it mean for domestic workers? Kimberly Amadeo of the *Balance* explains that the number of jobs that were sent overseas (14.3 million) was more than twice the number of unemployed workers in the United States (5.9 million) in 2015. Of course, Amadeo also points out that if these jobs were to return to the United States, it would mean that American workers would have to accept the lower wages that were offered to foreigner workers.[5] Another rebuke to this argument deals with the conditions of the jobs that tend to be sent abroad. They are often jobs at the lower end of the skill and wage spectrum. Will domestic workers be willing to take those jobs?

In terms of low wages, many believe that the job opportunities offered to workers in less developed countries is one of the most notable benefits of offshore manufacturing. They see it as a tool to alleviate global poverty. For instance, Mark Gunther of the *Guardian* cites that the steep decrease in extreme poverty in China—from 84 percent of the population to 10 percent—is largely due to global trade.[6] Moreover, DDD (Digital Divide Data)—a technology company—plans to use its data service centers in Cambodia, Kenya, and Laos as a means to help lift people out of poverty, offering training and other incentives beyond a salary.[5] Gunther also references Samasource, the Rockefeller Foundation, and Cloud Factory as companies that use outsourcing to help improve lives in other countries.[5] But does outsourcing offer long-term benefits to hosting countries, especially those that are underdeveloped?

The conditions of factories in developing countries—including sweatshops—have long been a source of controversy in the debate over offshore manufacturing. This controversy was vividly painted by the deadly collapse of the Rana Plaza in Bangladesh in 2013. The collapse of this building, which housed garment factories, resulted in the deaths and injuries of more than 1,000 people.[7] Even though this fatal accident led to changes in workers' safety regulations and practices, it showed how little attention is often given to workers' wellbeing. It also raised the question of whether offshore manufacturing is indeed just a way for companies to avoid strict and sometimes costly restrictions in countries with rigorous labor regulations.

Beyond arguments related to the financial benefits—or lack thereof—offered by offshore manufacturing, what does domestic and offshore manufacturing mean for the environment? The *Los Angeles Times* editorial board asserts that industrialized countries are the catalyst of the global climate change, though they will not be the ones to suffer most from its impacts.[8] However, many industrialized countries are now leading efforts to make better environmental decisions and reverse the negative environmental impacts caused by industrialization. In addition, as of 2019, the fight to prioritize the prevention of climate change has reached a boiling point, as demonstrated by events like the global school climate strikes originated by Greta Thunberg, a Swedish teenager and environmental activist. In 2015, the world saw an unprecedented accord—known as the Paris Climate Agreement— signed by 196 world leaders, which aimed to take necessary efforts to decrease our impact on the environment.[9] The environmental impacts of our choices—including those related to manufacturing—are now a greater source of concern and contemplation than ever before.

With these considerations in mind, there has recently been a greater focus on exploring the role offshore manufacturing plays in the climate change debate. For instance, how do companies dispose of hazardous materials in countries with few or lenient environmental regulations? Does moving operations offshore relieve companies of their environmental obligations, since often operations move to less developed countries where environmental regulations might be less rigorous? What are the environmental benefits of keeping operations on domestic soil, if any? After all, pollution is prevalent in industrialized countries as well as developing ones.

The debate over the economic advantages and disadvantages of domestic vs. offshore manufacturing is tied to many other issues, including workers' rights and safety and the environmental impacts of manufacturing on a national and global scale. There are numerous ways to argue for and against offshore manufacturing, and *Current Controversies: Domestic vs. Offshore Manufacturing* offers opposing viewpoints from experts that will help students better understand both sides of the debate and come to a more informed conclusion.

Notes

1. Christopher O'Leary, "Offshoring," *Encyclopedia Britannica*, n.d. https://www.britannica.com/topic/offshoring

2. "Labor Costs," US Department of Commerce, March 2018. https://acetool.commerce.gov/cost-risk-topic/labor-costs.

3. Bonnie Kavoussi, "Average Cost of a Factory Worker in the US, China and Germany," *HuffPost*, December 2016. https://www.huffpost.com/entry/average-cost-factory-worker_n_1327413.

4. "Labor Costs," US Department of Commerce, March 2018. https://acetool.commerce.gov/cost-risk-topic/labor-costs.

5. Kimberly Amadeo, "How Outsourcing Jobs Affects the US Economy," *The Balance*, July 2019. https://www.thebalance.com/how-outsourcing-jobs-affects-the-u-s-economy-3306279.

6. Marc Gunther, "Using Outsourcing to Help Alleviate Poverty in Africa and South Asia," *The Guardian*, June 2014. https://www.theguardian.com/sustainable-business/2014/jun/19/outsourcing-extreme-poverty-africa-south-asia-call-centres-ddd.

7. Nadra Nittle, "What the Rana Plaza Disaster Changed About Worker Safety," *Racked*, April 2018. https://www.racked.com/2018/4/13/17230770/rana-plaza-collapse-anniversary-garment-workers-safety.

8. The Times Editorial Board, "Editorial: Wealthy Countries Are Responsible For Climate Change, But It's The Poor Who Will Suffer Most," *Los Angeles Times*, September 2019. https://www.latimes.com/opinion/editorials/la-ed-climate-change-global-warming-part-2-story.html.

9. Camila Domonoske, "So What Exactly Is in the Paris Climate Accord?" *NPR*, June 2017. https://www.npr.org/sections/thetwo-way/2017/06/01/531048986/so-what-exactly-is-in-the-paris-climate-accord.

CHAPTER 1

Does Offshore Manufacturing Benefit Companies?

Overview: Different Factors Prove That the Debate Over Domestic vs. Offshore Manufacturing Is Complicated

Kimberly Amadeo

Kimberly Amadeo is an American economic expert who writes for both the Balance and the Dotdash publishing family. She also serves as the president of World Money Watch.

Job outsourcing is when US companies hire foreign workers instead of Americans. In 2015, US overseas affiliates employed 14.3 million workers. The four industries most affected are technology, call centers, human resources, and manufacturing.

How It Affects the Economy

Job outsourcing helps US companies be more competitive in the global marketplace. It allows them to sell to foreign markets with overseas branches. They keep labor costs low by hiring in emerging markets with lower standards of living. That lowers prices on the goods they ship back to the United States.

The main negative effect of outsourcing is it increases US unemployment. The 14.3 million outsourced jobs are more than double the 5.9 million unemployed Americans. If all those jobs returned, it would be enough to also hire the 4.3 million who are working part-time but would prefer full-time positions.

That assumes the jobs could, in fact, return to the United States. Many foreign employees are hired to help with local marketing, contacts, and language. It also assumes the unemployed here have the skills needed for those positions. Would American workers be willing to accept the low wages paid to foreign employees? If not, American consumers would be forced to pay higher prices.

"How Outsourcing Jobs Affects the US Economy," by Kimberly Amadeo, The Balance, Dotdash Publishing Family, July 23, 2019. Reprinted by permission.

Donald Trump said he would bring jobs back during the 2016 presidential campaign. To do this, he renegotiated NAFTA. He imposed tariffs on imports from Mexico and China. That started a trade war and raised the prices of imports from those countries. That benefits companies that make all their products in America. Without tariffs, it can be difficult for American-made goods to compete with cheaper foreign goods.

Imposing laws to artificially restrict job outsourcing could make US companies less competitive. If they are forced to hire expensive US workers, they would raise prices and increase costs for consumers.

The pressure to outsource might lead some companies to even move their whole operation, including headquarters, overseas. Others might not be able to compete with higher costs and would be forced out of business.

Technology Outsourcing

American companies send IT jobs to India and China because the skills are similar while the wages are much lower. A company only has to pay an entry-level IT worker $7,000 a year in China and $8,400 in India. Companies in Silicon Valley outsource tech jobs by offering H-1b visas to foreign-born workers.

Call Center Outsourcing

In the past 20 years, many call centers have been outsourced to India and the Philippines. That's because the workers there speak English. But that trend is changing. Unlike technology outsourcing, there is a much smaller wage discrepancy between call center workers in the United States and emerging markets.

Thanks to the Great Recession, wages in India began catching up to those in the United States. Average call center workers only make 15 percent more than their counterparts in India. As a result, some of these jobs are coming back.

Human Resources Outsourcing

Human resources outsourcing reduces costs by pooling thousands of businesses. This lowers the price of health benefit plans, retirement plans, workers' compensation insurance, and legal expertise. Human resource outsourcing particularly benefits small businesses by offering a wider range of benefits. Surprisingly, the recession may cause some human resource outsourcing firms to hire American workers.

NAFTA Job Losses

President Reagan envisioned NAFTA to help North America compete with the European Union. Unfortunately, it also sent at least 500,000 manufacturing jobs to Mexico. Hardest hit were California, New York, Michigan, and Texas.

Is Mexico Stealing US Jobs?

Mexico is now the seventh-largest auto manufacturer in the world. But did that growth come at the expense of US auto workers? Or is something else the real reason? Like 44 free trade agreements, perhaps?

Three Reasons India Attracts US Companies

India has three qualities that attract American companies. First, the labor force already speaks English. Second, its universities are among the highest-ranked in the world. Third, its legal system is similar to the United States, since both are rooted in the British system.

How China Takes US Jobs

China is the world's largest exporter. But a lot of China's so-called "exports" are really for American companies. A lot of US companies ship raw materials over, and the final goods are shipped back. One reason is that US companies can only afford to sell products to China's 1.37 billion people if they manufacture there.

Perhaps the United States should do the same thing. Imagine if all our imported products were partly manufactured in America?

Other foreign companies should be required to follow the lead of Japanese auto makers, who already do this. Of course, if the United States did that, it would mean higher prices for consumers. That's because US workers need a higher salary to pay for the better standard of living.

Are Robots a Bigger Threat than Outsourcing?

Workers in many manufacturing industries have been replaced by robots. To get new jobs, workers need training to operate the robots.

Innovations in technology are what actually allowed US companies to move call centers to India. If technology is the culprit, it is also the answer. It's made the United States more competitive as a nation. Education, rather than protectionism, is the best way to both take advantage of technology and create jobs for US workers.

Why You Feel Underpaid

One-quarter of American workers make less than $10 per hour, or are living in poverty. Meanwhile, the top 1 percent of workers earned more in income than the bottom 40 percent of workers. This was in 2005, when the economy was still booming. Outsourcing is just one reason. Technology, globalization and a passion for "low prices" above all else are others.

How to Find Jobs in the Freelance Economy

The freelance economy means that companies are laying off full-time, often older, workers and replacing them with part-timers, temp help, and freelance workers.

Can Trump Bring Back Americans Jobs?

President Trump focused his campaign on ending outsourcing to become the greatest job-producing president in US history. He promised to pressure China to reduce its subsidies and raise its currency value. He would renegotiate NAFTA to require Mexico to end the maquiladora program. He would lure companies back by reducing corporate taxes.

Companies Offshore to Stay Competitive

Diversify OSS

Diversify Offshore Staffing Solutions (Diversify OSS) is an Australia-based company that makes offshoring to the Philippines easier for companies by providing staffing and helping them achieve their goals.

Offshoring of services usually has negative connotations. Consumers fear that they will get less of what they paid for due to the low level of services the outsourced partner can provide. This may be depending on the country the service has been offshored to and its reliability of providing quality service or otherwise. Another reason is that the service provider uses a traditional outsourcing strategy wherein they are more focused on reaching the required metrics rather than focusing more on the quality of service they offer.

The Truth to Why Businesses Offshore

In a time where unemployment is prevalent across different countries, most people criticise companies that offshore their business operations. However, most fail to recognise that businesses face challenges that most non-business savvy people are not aware of or fully understand. In this article, we will be discussing some of the reasons why companies decide to offshore:

Cost

Businesses are constantly seeking different ways on how to gain a stable source of revenue while at the same time sustain their day-to-day operations to stay competitive or even survive. However, due to the unpredictable and excessive fluctuations in the economy, most companies cannot merely maintain the cost of local activities and that is why they turn to offshoring as a viable strategy. For

"Five Reasons Why Companies Offshore their Business," Diversify OSS, February 27, 2019. Reprinted by permission.

example, employing a local customer service representative in Australia costs an average of $60,000 a year while offshored salaries are almost a quarter of this price.

Through reducing overhead costs, businesses can redirect their resources to allow their local workforce to focus more on their core competencies, increase productivity, create more jobs and to prioritise revenue generating tasks.

Restrictive Regulation

One other concern that companies have to deal with are restrictive local regulations that hinder them from reaching long term business goals. Staying updated with local laws is vital for any business to operate continuously, but these regulations unintentionally cause added costs on operational expenses that later on leads to reducing competitiveness.

To Stay Competitive

In this interconnected world, businesses are now competing in a global stage wherein innovation is becoming a significant factor in determining the success of a company, and the constant demand for efficient customer service makes it more challenging for companies across different industries to stay relevant.

For a business to stay competitive, it needs to increase efficiency, enhance operational procedures and innovate on delivering quality service to their customers. Offshoring allows companies to offer highly valued services such as 24/7 customer support and provide effective service level tasks with flexible work schedules.

Quality

Offshoring specific back-office tasks can bring valuable results to your company. However, the quality of offshored services may vary from each country, and it will widely depend on the goals that your business aims to achieve. If the business is seeking to maximise its production, most companies will offshore their manufacturing to China. On the other hand, if the business wants to enhance their after sales support, offshoring customer service representatives in the Philippines will be the ideal solution. The talent and skill that the global workforce can offer is irreplaceable and should be effectively harnessed by companies to help them reach their long-term goals.

Companies must innovate on how to have an efficient process flow within their business for them to enhance the quality of their products and services. With the help of modern technology, companies now have full control over their offshore team thus enabling them to ensure quality in what they offer by making sure that offshored inputs meet their own quality standards.

Skill Shortage

The declining number of available job opportunities in different countries is one of the main reasons why most people disagree with companies offshoring their business operations. However, despite this situation, various industries are also struggling with how to overcome the rising number of skill shortage or by the lack of qualified staff to do the job.

In the United States, several government efforts were made in an attempt to bring back Apple's manufacturing jobs from China, but later on, failed due to the limited availability of local talent and infrastructure. According to recent reports, Apple confirmed that it would build their Mac Pro computer locally. However, the initiative faced staffing and supply problems early on, leading Apple to continue offshoring the rest of its products.

Australia is also experiencing the effects of skill shortage in the automotive industry. According to a recent labour market research survey for automotive trades, vacancies attracted an average of 0.8 suitable applicants per vacancy compared with 1.1 in 2016. The number of applicants per vacancy has been reported to be the lowest since 2008 while the proportion of jobs filled is the equal lowest since 2011. More than 20% of employers were unable to fill their vacancies despite attracting suitable applicants. Reasons for this included applicants rejecting offers of employment, location issues, working conditions, and the lack of willingness to do the job.

Through offshoring, companies discovered that they could hire a team of highly qualified staff in low-cost countries who are motivated and ready to take on tasks that are frequently rejected by local employees.

Redefining Offshoring

Offshoring remains to be a viable business strategy for many different reasons. However, like any other strategy, it is also prone to abuse and should not be used solely for cutting costs. Offshoring should not be seen as a replacement for your staff but instead, use it to augment your current team for further growth of your business. That is why this strategy needs to be carefully customised and tailor-fit with the company's needs without disrupting ongoing operations.

Outsourcing to China Helps Businesses Lower Their Production Costs

Nathan Resnick

Nathan Resnick is currently the CEO of Sourcify, a firm focused on connecting companies to offshored factories and streamlining the production process for them. He has also written for Entrepreneur *and* BigCommerce.

Chinese manufacturing is a practice that US and international businesses have recognized as an essential asset to reducing prices for their products. It's utilized by some of the most prominent brands and it has become a staple to successful manufacturing. As domestic prices rise, the need for affordable overseas manufacturing grows.

China has answered that call and today, you see the "Made in China" tagline on many custom products including clothing, furniture, and toys. Their manufacturing capabilities have continued to grow since the inception of China manufacturing, and their factories produce private label products worldwide. In 2002, China had over 80 million total employees in the manufacturing sector. By 2009, that number had grown to approximately 100 million. The United States, the next closest, maintained a steady decline in manufacturing employees through this period, with 15 million manufacturing employees by the end of 2009.

China has the lowest labor costs in the entire world for manufacturing employees. At the same time, it has grown an economy responsible for bringing more people out of poverty than any other country. Lower costs of living make China's low wages manageable for the common manufacturing worker, and their factories are thriving by producing goods for the entire world.

"The Advantages of Manufacturing in China and the Benefits It Brings to your Business," by Nathan Resnick, Sourcify, March 29, 2018. Reprinted by permission.

Sourcify and other companies help transition businesses to the profitable and successful move of manufacturing in China.

Lower Manufacturing Costs

The cost differential between manufacturing domestically and manufacturing in China is significant. Domestic manufacturers have higher overhead with steep training costs and high turnover. China's affordability makes overseas manufacturing ideal for the common business.

Cheaper Labor

Outsourcing to China gives you access to that factory's cheap labor without having to train the employees, provide access to a computer, or endure any of the other hardships of hiring locally. Wages are significantly lower in China and tapping into those savings is as easy as establishing a relationship with a factory.

Higher Production Capability

China-based factories produce goods for the global economy. They have scaled their manufacturing capabilities well beyond what was ever believed possible. When you outsource to China, you're working with time-tested factories that have been producing quality products in similar industries as yours for years on end, and in massive supply.

Better Expansion and Diversification Opportunities

Have you wanted to expand your business and offer new product lines or tap into upcoming markets, but didn't see that being possible through existing wholesalers? Outsourcing to China manufacturers allows you to do this on-the-fly. You can expand and diversify your product offerings, as well as sell your products to international markets much easier.

You Can Still Cut Lead Times

When you manufacture domestically, you become accustom to an immediate lead time. You're manufacturing on-site, so there's no real delay from when you place an order to when you receive it. This results in considerable savings because you can manufacture only the amount of stock that is needed, without over-manufacturing and eating into the budget.

This is often seen as a drawback of outsourcing the manufacturing process to an overseas provider. Your lead times are significantly increased, which means you might have to order more than is needed to account for the delay. However, with China manufacturers there are actually ways to cut lead times and experience quick deliveries of your product, which allows you to carry less stock and spend less.

Some of the ways you can do this include:

1. **Order more often.** By increasing the frequency in which you place orders, you will have a continuous supply of incoming product. Many factories have minimum order quantities, but they're often set at reasonable amounts or are negotiable by arranging for more frequent orders. By placing orders more often, you won't feel the pressures of low inventory and have a dire need to manufacture more product. This might be a more expensive approach since you won't get reduced bulk shipping, it will save your business money in carrying costs. Keeping too much supply on hand is a costly mistake that can be a damaging move to a startup.

2. **Send automated information.** When you place an order for product with your supplier, are there manual processes that must take place for the order to be approved? If you can, work on automating the delivery of that information. Whether it's a purchase order, invoice, or inventory sheet, start using software to automate the process. Inventory management software allows for auto purchase order generation and reorders once inventory levels reach a certain criterion.

3. **Share your data.** By providing your supplier with forecasts on inventory levels, you can allow them to track the same data and automate a purchase order on your behalf when needed. There are many suppliers that will happily integrate with your inventory management software and take the burden of monitoring SKUs and their inventory levels off your shoulders. Rather than having to expedite shipping for an order because inventory is low, the factory will already have kept tabs on the situation and done this for you.

Production Efficiency

Domestic manufacturing can be extremely expensive. Between labor and training costs, complications in the manufacturing process, and equipment costs, US and other mainland manufacturing companies must have considerable profit margins to manufacture at home successfully. These are industries such as aerospace, where profit is considerably high and sometimes even government-backed. Startups and businesses that are new to the industry have little chance of competing. China eliminates the high rate of failure that is so common in domestic manufacturing. Production efficiency is extremely high and because labor costs are affordable in China, complications like defects rarely derail the operation. Things can continue running smoothly and at little expense to your business.

Scam Prevention

One of the biggest concerns with manufacturing in China is the potential for being scammed. When you aren't working face-to-face, when there are language barriers, when the location of the factory is across an ocean, there's a tendency to grow worried. Companies like Sourcify actively work to protect businesses by connecting them with trusted and vetted overseas factories. You can immediately build a relationship and start outsourcing your manufacturing to China, without having to worry about being scammed or taken advantage of. Their system is a fool-proof way to get started that essentially guarantees you success in choosing a factory.

Product Duplication Capabilities

Is there a competing product that hit the nail on the head? You love what they did, you think it's fantastic, and you'd like to produce something similar for your own business. You don't want any legal trouble though, so you know it must be a duplicate and not an exact copy. China's product duplication capabilities are superior, and they can copy products at faster speed and with better accuracy than almost anywhere else. This is the exact process that made China the manufacturing kingpin to begin with. They used American and Japanese made products as inspiration and produce replicas that are essentially the same thing, but from materials that cost less and with a cheaper labor force. If you already have a working concept of a product you would like to rebrand manufacture for yourself, China's factories are a dependable and trustworthy place to make it happen.

Why Is Copycat Manufacturing Such a Big Deal?

Without the ability to duplicate an existing product and do it better and for less money, manufacturing would never evolve. It's the copycat culture that empowers the competition and allows for improvements. Quality may vary depending on the factory that implements the duplication, but one thing is for certain, it continues to improve with each iteration and becomes closer to exact resemblance of the real thing, or possibly even a better version. It's not uncommon at all to find a better quality and better priced replica from a China-based factory. Many times, the replica comes from the exact same factory as the original product.

Communicating and Negotiating with Factories

Traditionally, a drawback of working with an overseas supplier would be the language barrier and communication deficiency. Today, that barrier has almost been eliminated entirely.

With Skype and other communication technologies, there are many ways to get your message across and communicate with your factory of choice. You can send emails and text chats, talk through VOIP, connect on a conference call, share screens with voice chat, create videos, or use virtually any communication medium you wish. Most factories have English speaking representatives there to solve your problems and answer questions. They understand the need for a personalized experience.

Being able to negotiate with factories is another key advantage to China manufacturing. The competitive nature between factories means that you can shop for the most affordable and most responsive factory to produce your products. You have complete freedom to shop around, so-to-speak, and resources like Sourcify help put that power in your hands.

How to Find a Manufacturer

When it comes to manufacturing a new product in China, there is a reason that so many businesses choose Sourcify. It's one of the only tools that connects you with real, vetted factories, based in China, that have reputable histories with thousands of other entrepreneurs. It's a platform that enables products to go from the innovative stages of conception and modeling, to a genuine reality. You can create better products for your business and save time by working with an exclusive community of factories that are the real deal, not some fly-by-night operation.

Conclusion

If your business could benefit from lower manufacturing costs, China manufacturing might be the single best move your company could ever make. There are hundreds of quality suppliers established in China with real factories. Consider outsourcing your ideas or products overseas to get the most out of your business and improve your bottom line.

The Low Cost of Overseas Labor Often Outweighs Transportation Costs

Theo Anderson

Theo Anderson is a writer based in Chicago, Illinois. He writes for both the Columbia Business School and the Northwestern University Kellogg School of Management.

The cost of labor is an obvious and compelling reason to send jobs overseas. Low wages elsewhere are the main reason that about 5 million US manufacturing jobs were offshored between 2001 and 2011. About a third of them went to China.

But do low wages trump the negatives of offshoring, particularly the additional shipping time and associated transportation and hidden costs, like the overhead of managing suppliers who are far away?

Firms have begun asking that question more often and urgently as labor costs rise around the world. Wages have nearly doubled in China since 2008, for example. As a result, manufacturing jobs have begun to trickle back to the US. One survey in December 2015 found that 17 percent of manufacturing executives were already "reshoring" jobs—that is, bringing them back to the US. Another 37 percent were planning or considering it.

Labor costs are relatively easy to determine. But the other side of the equation— the cost of transporting goods from factories to the point of sale—involves trade-offs that make a reliable cost–benefit analysis hard to come by.

"It's not just about the dollar cost of labor," says Jan Van Mieghem, a professor of operations at the Kellogg School. "Time is money, and firms have become smarter in realizing that, 'well,

"How Much Does It Cost to Manufacture Overseas vs. At Home?" by Theo Anderson, Kellogg Insight, July 10, 2017. Previously published in Kellogg Insight. Reprinted with permission of the Kellogg School of Management.

we can go to China, but it's going to take a longer time to get the product back here. And I will pay for that time.'"

Van Mieghem and his coauthor Robert Boute, of the University of Leuven, have developed a formula based on a model they designed that helps companies weigh a broad range of factors in deciding whether it makes sense to offshore jobs, manufacture locally, or do a mix of both, which is known as "dual sourcing."

"If I'm making sourcing decisions, I need to quantify it," Van Mieghem says of the choice between manufacturing overseas, manufacturing nearby, or relying on some mix of the two. "This model is one of the first that gives the quantifiable impact."

Both Sides Now

Van Mieghem's formula will be especially useful to companies in volatile markets, where demand shifts rapidly. These markets create uncertainty and force companies into a dilemma as they analyze which sourcing approach makes sense.

"You can keep a lot of product in inventory, which will cost you money," says Van Mieghem. "And you may end up having too much on hand. Or you can be more conservative and keep less in inventory. But then you run the risk that you won't have enough on hand, and customers will go elsewhere."

Manufacturing nearby means a company can keep inventory levels low but still get goods to market quickly when demand spikes. But does that benefit outweigh the cost of paying higher wages?

The answer depends in part on the costs of ramping up production to meet surges in demand—known as "capacity costs." If a supplier usually produces 100 units per day, for example, and demand rises to 150 units per day, how quickly can it meet the demand for 50 additional units, and at what cost?

In a word, how *flexible* is the supplier?

"The more expensive it is to pay overtime, hire extra workers, run weekend shifts and extra shifts, the more inflexible you are from a capacity perspective," Van Mieghem says.

European economies tend to be highly regulated and have high rates of unionization. The same is true, to a lesser extent, in some parts of the US. This inflexibility has driven the offshoring of so many jobs over the past several decades.

The formula developed by Van Mieghem and Boute helps a firm weigh these capacity flexibility costs against the benefits of sourcing nearby, such as the reduction in import taxes and inventory costs. Without the benefit of such a formula, it has been tempting for decision makers to fixate on the low cost of labor abroad.

"In the past, companies kind of underestimated, or neglected, the costs of the time it takes to transport goods, and the cost of needing more inventory," Van Mieghem says. "And many companies have become more aware of this. So they're in a mode of not relying completely on low-cost, faraway sourcing. They realize that they need some nearby sourcing, too."

Van Mieghem's formula helps them determine the right balance. A firm can input its own data on wage costs and capital investments, capacity costs, lead time, and so on to determine the optimal mix of sourcing abroad and nearby. Van Mieghem is now consulting with a major computer company to apply his formula to its products.

The formula can also be applied to shipping costs, helping a firm choose the best mix of transporting goods by ocean and by air, and it can help determine the optimal mix of local sources, not just local and offshore sources.

Bringing It (Partly) Back Home

The lure of low wages is especially strong in the realm of computers and electronics, an industry distinguished by strong competition and low profit margins.

But technology firms are the classic case of an industry that can benefit from dual sourcing. Demand for computers and cell phones, and the related devices and accessories, is highly volatile—making them prime candidates for nearby sourcing. The cost of labor may be higher, but companies save on shipping. They are also able to keep inventories low while offering rapid delivery, which technology consumers tend to value.

Those advantages are one reason the US has gained some manufacturing jobs in the past few years, after three decades of steady offshoring. For example, the Chinese computer manufacturer Lenovo opened a new factory in 2013 in North Carolina.

That state has had another recent win in terms of keeping sourcing local from a different sector: furniture manufacturing. It is home to nearly 10 percent of all the jobs in furniture manufacturing in the US, and has begun to win back some of those jobs it lost over the past few decades.

The industry's strategy for doing so has involved, in part, becoming smarter about inventory management and maximizing the advantages of making furniture in factories closer to showrooms. That strategy substantially reduces both the costs of storing furniture and the administrative costs of tracking it to the point of sale.

Despite such advantages of manufacturing nearby, the low cost of labor means that offshoring or dual sourcing still makes economic sense for many companies. Van Mieghem's formula can help companies understand how to plan their sourcing in the current market—and years down the road. "It can be used as a planning model, to project out for the next few years what you believe should happen with your global footprint. Should we keep investing more and more in Asia—or should we start investing more over here?"

Offshoring Affects Wages in the US Market

Adam Hersh and Ethan Gurwitz

Adam Hersh and Ethan Gurwitz both work at the Center for American Progress, where Hersh serves as a senior economist and Gurwitz serves as a research assistant.

The global economy is becoming a more integrated and competitive neighborhood. Driven by new investments and the jobs that come with them, the expansion of the global economy into coordinated production and supply chains brings both benefits and opportunities. It also raises questions about the source and location of future jobs and growth.

Offshoring, the practice of moving production to foreign locales while continuing to sell goods to the US market, is a pervasive feature of the US economy today. Market pressures drive businesses to seek reduced production costs, often in places where standards of living and protections for workers and the environment are more lax than in the United States. Moreover, an ineffective tax structure further encourages the relocation of assets and production to foreign countries with lower costs. Policies such as a tax credit that reduces the costs a company incurs when it reshores jobs back to the United States would help slow this trend. In addition, the financial incentive to bring production back would help workers here at home, where production loss has led to broad downward pressure on wages across the economy, even in industries relatively insulated from international trade competition.

Offshoring is a prevalent feature of the US economy, with much of this trade occurring within multinational companies' corporate families. As is clear from the data on US goods imports driven by trade between related corporate entities from 2002 to 2013, the share of products imported to the United States from related

"Offshoring Work Is Taking a Toll on the US Economy," by Adam Hersh and Ethan Gurwitz, Center for American Progress, July 30, 2014. Reprinted by permission.

corporate entities constitutes nearly half of all US imports since 2004. As more businesses moved production to lower-cost regions, this share increased to 50 percent in 2013, up from 48 percent in 2004.

When looking specifically at the manufacturing sector, imports for capital-intensive industries such as machinery and chemicals—primary drivers of productivity growth and innovation—illustrate the hollowing out of US industry through their disproportionately high share of trade between related corporate entities relative to the overall economy average. Paradoxically, US companies were much less likely to engage in production relocation in low-capital and low-skill, labor-intensive manufacturing industries over the past decade, indicating that US and global businesses see the US market more as a destination for sales than as place to invest in production.

In comparison to US imports, the related-party exports shown as a share of overall US exports indicate that offshoring is a two-way street. Multinational companies from other countries are locating production in the United States for sale in other countries' markets but are doing so at a much lower rate than the US-based companies locating production offshore to supply goods to the US market.

In reality, offshoring is an even more pervasive phenomenon than is displayed here as these data capture only the related-party aspects of the practice. Outsourcing—offshoring through arms-length contractual relationships between separate entities—is common as well.

The recent rising US surplus in services trade—particularly financial and legal services and licensing income from intellectual properties—also reflects the offshoring phenomenon, not merely the competitive strength of US service industries. Data from the Bureau of Economic Analysis show the share of trade in services exports that occurs within related corporate entities. Starting around 1993, the share of US service exports to related corporate entities began to grow, reaching nearly 68 percent of overall service exports in 2011. This was up from around 45 percent in 1987. The trend is clear: As offshoring practices increase, companies need to provide more wraparound services—the things needed to run a businesses besides direct production—to their offshore production and research and development activities. Rather than indicating the competitive strength of US services businesses to expand abroad, the growth in services exports follows the pervasive offshoring of manufacturing and commercial research activities.

The United States tax code actually incentivizes moving production, jobs, and profits overseas by favoring overseas investment with a lower effective tax rate. According to a Tax Law Review article by Melissa Costa and Jennifer G. Gravelle, foreign-source income for US multinational corporations saw an average tax rate of 15.7 percent as of 2007, while domestic-based income saw an average rate of 26 percent, a disparity of around 10 percentage points. As noted in a Center for American Progress report on corporate tax reform, this distortion in the tax treatment of foreign and domestic corporate income "violates economic neutrality and does not serve our national interest."

Finally, offshoring and import competition are taking a toll on wages in the United States. Recent research from Michael Elsby of the University of Edinburgh, Bart Hobijn of the Federal Reserve Bank of San Francisco, and Aysegul Sahin of the Federal Reserve Bank of New York shows that the more a US industry is exposed to offshoring pressures, the more downward pressure is put on the wage share within it. The authors show that this wage effect, steadily building over the past 25 years, has been felt broadly across the economy even—though less intensely—in non-import-competing industries.

As is evident from the data above, increased economic competition, market pressures, and an ineffective tax system have resulted in an increase in the practice of moving production to offshore locales and then selling goods back to the US market. Policies such as a tax credit that reduces the costs of reshoring jobs back to the United States would go far to ameliorate this trend. Similarly, a tax credit could help slow the growing negative pressure on wages evident in most import-competing industries.

Offshore Manufacturing Costs Companies More Than Expected

Global Manufacturing Services, Inc.

Global Manufacturing Services, Inc. is a woman-owned contract manufacturer that specializes in electronic manufacturing services.

A few weeks ago, I had the pleasure of sitting down and speaking with a couple of gentlemen who collectively had more than 60 years' experience in a global industry. In the early years of their business, they were able to use domestic suppliers for everything, but as competition in their space grew, prices were driven down, and they like many other original equipment manufacturers, found it necessary to source product components overseas.

During our conversation, they shared a notable nugget of information about their organization's experience with offshore sourcing. As the company began sourcing overseas, they also started monitoring the procurement process and the associated costs for overseas and domestic suppliers. Of course, they could easily compare component pricing, shipping costs, and other readily available costs, but they also tracked the hidden costs that are often merely rolled into an organization's overhead expenses. Things like the time their staff invested in the procurement process. The investment in increased inventory levels, which protected against longer lead times. They even considered the cost of capital for advanced payments to overseas manufacturers vs. their domestic payment terms. They monitored every action taken from the moment the order demands were triggered until the components reached their destination.

The years of data painted a clear picture. When considering the entire buying process, they determined that overseas sourcing added, on average, 27% more to these hidden expenses. The company

"What is the Real Cost of Offshore Manufacturing?" Global Manufacturing Services, Inc., January 1, 2018. Reprinted by permission.

can now assess the offshore manufacturing costs accurately. While foreign manufacturers usually offer much better pricing, this organization can see the real costs of the offshore option by adding in the 27%. In many cases, the overseas option still provides significant savings, but at least this organization understands their costs, and they are confident in their buying decisions.

So how should their story change how we all look at offshore manufacturing? Glad you ask. Their story peeked my curiosity. As a bit of a self-proclaimed "Biznologist," and no, that is not a word, but maybe it should be. I define "biznologist" as someone who is a business geek and loves to study business models, strategy, behavior, … someone who likes peeling back the layers of business. In my 30 plus years of business analysis, I have spoken to a number of representative companies who source products outside of the US. They all share some form of this assertion, "you cannot compete without low-cost overseas manufacturing." They also admit to not knowing the hidden costs associated with the practice. They merely focus on the product costs, shipping costs, and lead times.

My thought processes led me to break down each phase of the buying process, discover the typical issues associated with each, and compare the pros and cons of domestics and offshore options. I also assumed the years of data collected by this respected organization provided enough evidence to reasonably conclude the additional hidden costs of 27% would be in the range of statistical norms. If your company has data that validates or refutes their findings, I would love to hear from you. For now, I will assume this case falls within the normal statistical range and is not an outlier.

After considerable research and thought, my conclusion was that there are several areas we should consider when evaluating offshore manufacturing, and any or all of them may add hidden costs to the procurement process. Of course, the specific costs associated with each area may differ from one organization to the other, but it will be helpful to consider each area as you make sourcing choices.

Intellectual Property (IP) Concerns

This topic undoubtedly deserves much more attention, but here we will just provide a 30 thousand foot view. Is your product significantly superior to similar products? If so, will your product sales be depressed by a knockoff? Obviously, if your product offers excellent product benefits, you should be able to charge a premium price for the product. So, protecting your IP may be more important than reducing your manufacturing costs. Since IP concerns increase drastically with offshore manufacturing, you will have to weigh the risk and decide which direction is more palatable and which strategy fits your product and organizational goals.

Cost of Inventory

To get significant price breaks, will you have to order 3, 6 or 12 months' supply? Consider the costs associated with the capital investment made in inventory; additional space required for storage, and even the human capital necessary to warehouse and manage the product. We often absorb these costs into our overhead, but if we estimate the additional warehouse square footage and workforce needed to maintain the excess inventory, we can then apply it to the costs of the products represented. The numbers can be staggering, and there may be a better solution.

Cost of Inventory Management

Because of longer lead times for overseas manufacturing, do you have to increase your inventory levels to protect against "out of stock" items? Most companies wrestle with inventory levels. The fluctuations in demand, coupled with raw material availability, manufacturing delays, damaged goods, deficient goods … all make it challenging to manage lean inventory levels. Since the cost of missed sales opportunities is too costly to measure adequately, most companies err on the side of too much product. So, consider how you may utilize a domestic supplier to help. Can they act as a more agile primary, or secondary supplier, allowing you to reduce inventory levels, warehouse size, and staff while preserving your ability to fill orders as customers expect?

Time Zone Inefficiencies

Managing manufacturing projects on the other side of the world has challenges. Often time we are forced to schedule conference calls late at night. When we communicate via email, it is usually several hours before the recipient sees it, and their response often comes in the middle of the night. You then get it and respond when they are asleep. An inefficient communication cycle like this can slow the production process down considerably. The only way to avoid delays is to make sure someone is available 24/7 from both companies. Of course, many companies hire employees and base them in the manufacturer's country to manage production. Others outsource the work to a broker. In every case, there are added costs to the process, and they must be considered part of the cost of your offshore program.

Additional Time Required to Manage Manufacturing

Coupled with the time zone delays and extra time invested after hours, is the added time needed to communicate clearly. A five-minute production discussion with a colleague can become an hour-long conversation with someone speaking English as a second language. Some companies address this by hiring a bilingual employee, and it can be a cost-effective option if you have a steady flow of manufacturing projects. Again, consider the costs.

Product Damage or Loss in Transition

Most domestic manufacturers, own the product until you receive it in your warehouse. Most overseas manufacturers work differently. Ownership of the product transfers when it leaves their plant, so any damages or missing product during transition becomes your responsibility. There are typically options available for recouping the loss but do not expect anything to happen quickly. Not to mention, if you need the inventory, you have to jump through hoops to get more on the way. We have to think about such issues and consider their associated risk and costs.

Advanced Payment Requirements

Unless you have a long-standing, trusted relationship with your overseas manufacturer, you will be required to pay in advance for your goods.

In most cases, offshore manufacturers will not ship product until payment is received. In cases where you transport goods via the water, your payment is processed 30 days or more before you get your product. As you know, there is a cost to paying 30 days before you have the product, especially when compared to 30-day terms with a domestic manufacturer. There is a minimum of a 60-day difference between the two options. If you are paying from existing cash-flow, it may not be too bad. If not, add the costs of capital for at least the 60 days. You may want to track your payment date and received dates to determine precisely how many days of the capital cost to add. It may not seem like it is worth monitoring, but as you combine all the possible added expenditures, it may tell a compelling story.

The Risk When Initially Sourcing

The costs incurred while getting your overseas program started can be staggering. The search for the right manufacturer, and learning the ins and out of the process will be costly, even if you hire someone with good experience. Most companies address this by hiring a consultant, or a broker to assist in the process. We rarely consider the ROI of transitioning from domestic to overseas manufacturing, but the time/labor costs are usually significant.

Insufficient Legal Recourse

Lastly, insufficient legal recourse is one of the most significant risks to consider. What are your options, if things go wrong? Whether you are dealing with a domestic or offshore manufacturer, something will eventually go south. Most of the time a reasonable and equitable solution can be found, and you move on. Unfortunately, there are instances when things do not go well, and a realistic solution seems tenuous at best. In such cases, US companies doing business overseas will often elect to write off the loss and sever their relationship with the overseas manufacturer. There are no good legal options available and cutting ties, while justifiable, creates additional expenses. You have to locate and onboard a new manufacturer. How long will it take to groom the new team? Do I have enough supply to get through the re-start phase? Do you have a secondary supplier, overseas, or domestically? If not, it is a worthwhile pursuit.

There is a lot to consider when sourcing manufacturing partners and this article only scratches the surface, but I hope it may inspire you to take a fresh look at the real costs and potential risk.

Offshoring Leads to Product Recalls

Robert Handfield

Robert Handfield serves as the executive director of the Supply Chain Resource Cooperative and as a Bank of America University Distinguished Professor of Supply Chain Management at North Carolina State University.

Over the last two decades, increased competition and a globalized economy has led firms to deploy outsourced manufacturing and captive offshore policies across multiple industries. Enterprises have sought to achieve reduced production costs and labor arbitrage in the quest for cost competitiveness. However, in the rush to source globally from low cost countries, the risk of product quality defects resulting in products recalls has often been overlooked by supply chain managers. This was the topic of a recent paper I worked on with Manfredi Bruccoleri from the University of Palermo.

This is starting to change…quickly! The increase in the number of product recalls in recent years has been attributed to higher levels of outsourcing and captive offshoring of manufacturing and distribution. Examples of recalls in 2016 alone span many products, including cell phones (Samsung Galaxy), automobiles (Volkswagen), bicycles (Trek), kitchen products (Cuisinart), computer batteries, toys (Toys R Us), faucets, lightbulbs, tools, pharmaceutical products and multiple other products.

Globalized supply chains have presented multiple unexpected challenges for executives, including delays in product sourcing, distribution issues, and quality defects. These events may occur for a number of reasons, including poor communication due to geographical distance between customer and supplier, diversity of regulatory standards, socio-cultural diversity, and complexity in

"Is Offshoring Leading to Increased Numbers of Product Recalls?" by Robert Handfield, North Carolina State University, January 4, 2017. Reprinted by permission.

coordinating and exchanging information between different actors. For example, in the pharmaceutical industry, a typical supply chain design consisting of sourcing, manufacturing, packaging and distribution occurring in disparate global locations globally. This supply chain design has increased the risk of contamination or substitution of active ingredients, as in the case of the 2008 heparin incident.[1] In the toy industry, some researchers argue that poor product quality of toys produced in China may not be due to the poor quality of Chinese manufacturing, but rather by the long and more complex supply chains that lead to poor oversight. In a domestic supply chain, the brand owner designs the product and develops procedures for internal manufacturing, storing, and distribution, and defines the standards for quality control and testing. In extended complex supply chains it becomes more difficult to guarantee that every supply chain actor understands and complies with procedures at every node, from raw materials to the point of sale. This gap in communication of requirements increases the risk of product quality failure and product recall, especially in cases where the company is not well versed in global sourcing.

One fact remains certain; the trend of outsourcing and offshoring manufacturing is not likely to abate anytime soon. With Trump's call to limit global sourcing imports into the US, the global offshoring model may be at risk for a number of different reasons. Despite research pointing to offshore manufacturing as the primary root cause for recalls (there is actually very little in the scientific literature that explores how enterprises should respond to product quality failures that result in a recall. Direct product recall costs are a function of the number and dimension of the lots to be withdrawn from the market, as well as the resilience of the supply chain structural design to cope with the damage (costs) inflicted by the recall. Upon learning of a product quality failure, the ability of a supply chain organization to dampen the magnitude/severity of the disruption (e.g. the volume of product recalls) can directly reduce the costs of recalls.

The extent to which an enterprise responds well or poorly to a product recall event is a relevant question, as product markets continue to experience product recalls on a regular basis. For example, the cost for repairing the vehicles involved in General Motors' recall crisis in the first three months of 2014 was about $1.3 billion, and involved more than 6 million cars worldwide produced since 2002.[2] Why were so many cars involved in the recall? Why was General Motors' so unprepared for such a disruption? How much would GM have saved shareholders if its supply chain had been more resilient, and could have minimized the number of vehicles impacted by the recall?

People are increasingly beginning to argue that global sourcing increases the complexity of the supply chain and contributes to the severity of supply chain disruptions. In applying this rationale, it may well be that offshore outsourcing and captive offshoring negatively impacts an organization's product recall resilience.

Notes

1. China and US clash over cause of heparin deaths. Bloomberg.com. 21-Apr-2008 www.bloomberg.com/apps/news?pid=newsarchive&sid=aUAE9VN4.xX0&refer=home# accessed May 12, 2011.

2. CBS News. General Motors announces 30th recall of year. 23-May-2014 www.cbsnews.com/news/general-motors-announces-30th-recall-of-year

CHAPTER 2

Does Offshore Manufacturing Help the Economies of Developing Countries?

Overview: Doing Business Overseas Requires a Greater Understanding of the Local Culture

Rice University

Rice University is a private research university based in Houston, Texas. It was founded in 1891 by the American businessman William Marsh Rice.

It has been said that English is the language of money and, for that reason, has become the language of business, finance, trade, communication, and travel. As such, English carries with it the values and assumptions of its native speakers around the world. But not all cultures share these assumptions, at least not implicitly. The sick leave or vacation policies of a British investment bank, for instance, may vary greatly from those of a shoe manufacturer in Laos. Because business and capitalism as conducted today have evolved primarily from European origins and profits are measured against Western standards like the US dollar, the ethics that emerges from them is also beholden primarily (but not exclusively) to Western conceptions of behavior. The challenge for business leaders everywhere is to draw out the values of local cultures and integrate the best of those into their management models. The opportunities for doing so are enormous given the growing impact of China, India, Russia, and Brazil in global commerce. The cultures of these countries will affect the dominant business model, possibly even defining new ethical standards.

Business Encounters Culture

To understand the influence of culture on business ethics, it is essential to understand the concepts of enculturation and acculturation. In its most basic anthropological sense, enculturation refers to the process by which humans learn the rules, customs, skills, and values to participate in a society. In other words, no

"The Relationship Between Business Ethics and Culture," by Rice University, BC Campus, https://opentextbc.ca/businessethicsopenstax/chapter/the-relationship-between-business-ethics-and-culture/. Licensed under CC BY 4.0.

one is born with culture; all humans, regardless of their origin, have to learn what is considered appropriate behavior in their surrounding cultures. Whereas enculturation is the acquisition of any society's norms and values, acculturation refers specifically to the cultural transmission and socialization process that stems from cultural exchange. The effects of this blending of cultures appear in both the native (original) culture and the host (adopted) culture. Historically, acculturation has often been the result of military or political conquest. Today, it also comes about through economic development and the worldwide reach of the media.

One of the earliest real estate deals in the New World exemplifies the complexity that results when different cultures, experiences, and ethical codes come into contact. No deed of sale remains, so it is difficult to tell exactly what happened in May 1626 in what is now Manhattan, but historians agree that some kind of transaction took place between the Dutch West India Company, represented by Pieter Minuit, the newly appointed director-general of the New Netherland colony, and the Lenape, a Native American tribe. Which exact Lenape tribe is unknown; its members may have been simply passing through Manhattan and could have been the Canarsee, who lived in what is today southern Brooklyn.

Legend has it that the Dutch bought Manhattan island for $24 worth of beads and trinkets, but some historians believe the natives granted the Dutch only fishing and hunting rights and not outright ownership. Furthermore, the price, acknowledged as "sixty guilders" (about $1000 today), could actually represent the value of items such as farming tools, muskets, gun powder, kettles, axes, knives, and clothing offered by the Dutch. Clearly, the reality was more nuanced than the legend.

The "purchase" of Manhattan is an excellent case study of an encounter between two vastly different cultures, worldviews, histories, and experiences of reality, all within a single geographic area. Although it is a misconception that the native peoples of what would become the United States did not own property or value individual possession, it is nevertheless true that their approach to property was more fluid than that of the Dutch and of later settlers like the English, who regarded property as a fixed commodity that could be owned and transferred to others. These differences, as well as enforced taxation, eventually led to war between the Dutch and several Native American tribes.

European colonization only exacerbated hostilities and misunderstandings, not merely about how to conduct business but also about how to live together in harmony.

For more information, read this article about the Manhattan purchase and the encounter between European and Native American cultures and also this article about Peter Minuit and his involvement. What unexamined assumptions by both parties led to problems between them?

Two major conditions affect the relationship between business and culture. The first is that business is not culturally neutral. Today, it typically displays a mindset that is Western and primarily English-speaking and is reinforced by the enculturation process of Western nations, which tends to emphasize individualism and competition. In this tradition, business is defined as the exchange of goods and services in a dedicated market for the purpose of commerce and creating value for its owners and investors. Thus, business is not open ended but rather directed toward a specific goal and supported by beliefs about labor, ownership, property, and rights.

In the West, we typically think of these beliefs in Western terms. This worldview explains the misunderstanding between Minuit, who assumed he was buying Manhattan, and the tribal leaders, who may have had in mind nothing of the sort but instead believed they were granting some use rights. The point is that a particular understanding of and approach to business are already givens in any particular culture. Businesspeople who work across cultures in effect have entered the theater in the middle of the movie, and often they must perform the translation work of business to put their understanding and approach into local cultural idioms. One example of this is the fact that you might find *sambal* chili sauce in an Indonesian McDonald's in place of Heinz ketchup, but the restaurant, nevertheless, is a McDonald's.

The second condition that affects the relationship between business and culture is more complex because it reflects an evolving view of business in which the purpose is not solely generating wealth but also balancing profitability and responsibility to the public interest and the planet. In this view, which has developed as a result of political change and economic globalization, organizations comply with legal and economic regulations but then go beyond them to effect social change and sometimes even social justice.

The dominant manufacture-production-marketing-consumption model is changing to meet the demands of an increasing global population and finite resources. No longer can an organization maintain a purely bottom-line mentality; now it must consider ethics, and, therefore, social responsibility and sustainability, throughout its entire operation. As a result, local cultures are assuming a more aggressive role in defining their relationship with business prevalent in their regions.

Had this change taken place four centuries ago, that transaction in Manhattan might have gone a little differently. However, working across cultures can also create challenging ethical dilemmas, especially in regions where corruption is commonplace. A number of companies have experienced this problem, and globalization will likely only increase its incidence.

If you were to do a top-ten list of the world's greatest corruption scandals, the problems of Petrobras (*Petróleo Brasiliero*) in Brazil surely would make the list. The majority state-owned petroleum conglomerate was a party to a multibillion-dollar scandal in which company executives received bribes and kickbacks from contractors in exchange for lucrative construction and drilling contracts. The contractors paid Petrobras executives upward of five percent of the contract amount, which was funneled back into slush funds. The slush funds, in turn, paid for the election campaigns of certain members of the ruling political party, *Partido dos Trabalhadores*, or Workers Party, as well as for luxury items like race cars, jewelry, Rolex watches, yachts, wine, and art.

The original investigation, known as Operation Car Wash (*Lava Jato*), began in 2014 at a gas station and car wash in Brasília, where money was being laundered. It has since expanded to include scrutiny of senators, government officials, and the former president of the republic, Luiz Inácio Lula da Silva. The probe also contributed to the impeachment and removal of Lula's successor, Dilma Rousseff. Lula and Rousseff are members of the Workers Party. The case is complex, revealing Chinese suppliers, Swiss bank accounts where money was hidden from Brazilian authorities, and wire transfers that went through New York City and caught the eye of the US Department of Justice. In early 2017, the Brazilian Supreme Court justice in charge of the investigation and prosecution was mysteriously killed in a plane crash.

It is hard to imagine a more tragic example of systemic breakdown and individual vice. The loss of trust in government and the economy still affects ordinary Brazilians. Meanwhile, the investigation continues.

Balancing Beliefs

What about the ethical dimensions of a business in a developed country engaging in commerce in an environment where corruption might be more rampant than at home? How can an organization remain true to its mission and what it believes about itself while honoring local customs and ethical standards? The question is significant because it goes to the heart of the organization's values, its operations, and its internal culture. What must a business do to engage with local culture while still fulfilling its purpose, whether managers see that purpose as profitability, social responsibility, or a balance between the two?

Most business organizations hold three kinds of beliefs about themselves. The first identifies the purpose of business itself. In recent years, this purpose has come to be the creation not just of shareholder wealth but also of economic or personal value for workers, communities, and investors.

The second belief defines the organization's mission, which encapsulates its purpose. Most organizations maintain some form of mission statement. For instance, although IBM did away with its formal mission statement in 2003, its underlying beliefs about itself have remained intact since its founding in 1911. These are (1) dedication to client success, (2) innovation that matters (for IBM and the world), and (3) trust and personal responsibility in all relationships.

President and chief executive officer (CEO) Ginni Rometty stated the company "remain[s] dedicated to leading the world into a more prosperous and progressive future; to creating a world that is fairer, more diverse, more tolerant, more just."

Johnson & Johnson was one of the first companies to write a formal mission statement, and it is one that continues to earn praise. This statement has been embraced by several succeeding CEOs at the company, illustrating that a firm's mission statement can have a value that extends beyond its authors to serve many generations of managers and workers. Read Johnson & Johnson's mission statement to learn more.

Finally, businesses also go through the process of enculturation; as a result, they have certain beliefs about themselves, drawn from the customs, language, history, religion, and ethics of the culture in which they are formed. One example of a company whose ethics and ethical practices are deeply embedded in its culture is Merck & Co., one of the world's largest pharmaceutical companies and known for its strong ethical values and leadership. As its founder George W. Merck (1894–1957) once stated, "We try to remember that medicine is for the patient. We try never to forget that medicine is for the people. It is not for the profits. The profits follow, and if we have remembered that, they have never failed to appear. The better we have remembered it, the larger they have been."

Culture is deeply rooted, but businesses may make their own interpretations of its accepted norms.

Merck & Co. is justly lauded for its involvement in the fight to control the spread of river blindness in Africa. For more information, watch this World Bank video about Merck & Co.'s efforts to treat river blindness and its partnership with international organizations and African governments.

Our beliefs are also challenged when a clash occurs between a legal framework and cultural norms, such as when a company feels compelled to engage in dubious and even illegal activities to generate business. For example, the German technology company Siemens has paid billions of dollars in fines and judgments for bribing government officials in several countries. Although some local officials may have expected to receive bribes to grant government contracts, Siemens was still bound by national and international regulations forbidding the practice, as well as by its own code of ethics. How can a company remain true to its mission and code of ethics in a highly competitive international environment?

Ethical decision-making in a global context requires a broad perspective. Business leaders need to know themselves, their organization's mission, and the impact of their decisions on local communities. They also must be open to varying degrees of risk.

Business performance is a reflection of what an organization believes about itself, as in the IBM and Merck examples.

Those beliefs, in turn, spring from what the individuals in the organization believe about it and themselves, based on their communities, families, personal biographies, religious beliefs, and educational backgrounds. Unless key leaders have a vision for the organization and themselves, and a path to achieving it, there can be no balance of beliefs about profitability and responsibility, or integration of business with culture. The Manhattan purchase was successful to the degree that Minuit and the tribal leaders were willing to engage in an exchange of mutual benefit. Yet this revealed a transaction between two very different commercial cultures. Did each group truly understand the other's perception of an exchange of goods and services? Furthermore, did the parties balance personal and collective beliefs for the greater good? Given the distinctions between these two cultures, would that even have been possible?

Consumerism and the Global Marketplace

To paraphrase the ancient Greek philosopher Heraclitus (c. 535–475 BCE), the one constant in life is change. Traditional norms and customs have changed as the world's population has grown more diverse and urbanized, and as the Internet has made news and other resources readily available. The growing emphasis on consumerism—a lifestyle characterized by the acquisition of goods and services—has meant that people have become defined as "consumers" as opposed to citizens or human beings. Unfortunately, this emphasis eventually leads to the problem of diminishing marginal utility, with the consumer having to buy an ever-increasing amount to reach the same level of satisfaction. At the same time, markets have become more diverse and interconnected. For example, South Korean companies like LG and Samsung employ 52,000 workers in the United States, and many US companies now manufacture their products abroad. Such globalization of their domestic markets has allowed US consumers to enjoy products from around the world, but it also presents ethical challenges. The individual consumer, for instance, may benefit from lower prices and a greater selection of goods, but only by supporting a company that might be engaged in unethical practices in its overseas supply or distribution chains. Producers' choices about wages, working conditions, environmental impact, child labor, taxation, and plant safety feature in the creation of each product brought to market. Becoming aware of these factors requires consumers to engage in an investigation of the business practices of those parties they will patronize and exercise a certain amount of cultural and ethical sensitivity.

Overseas Manufacturing

How can the purchase of a pair of sneakers be seen as an ethical act? Throughout the 1990s, the US shoe and sportswear manufacturer Nike was widely criticized for subcontracting with factories in China and Southeast Asia that were little more than sweatshops with deplorable working conditions. After responding to the criticisms and demanding that its suppliers improve their workplaces, the company began to redeem itself in the eyes of many and has become a model of business ethics and sustainability. However, questions remain about the relationship between business and government.

For instance, should a company advocate for labor rights, a minimum wage, and unionization in developing countries where it has operations? What responsibility does it have for the welfare of a contractor's workers in a culture with differing customs? What right does any Western company have to insist that its foreign contractors observe in their factories the protocols required in the West? What, for example, is sacred about an eight-hour workday? When Nike demands that foreign manufacturers observe Western laws and customs about the workplace, arguably this is capitalist imperialism. Not only that, but Western firms will be charged more for concessions regarding factory conditions. Perhaps this is as it should be, but Western consumers must then be prepared to pay more for material goods than in the past.

Some argue that demanding that companies accept these responsibilities imposes cultural standards on another culture through economic pressure. Others insist there should be universal standards of humane employee treatment, and that they must be met regardless of where they come from or who imposes them. But should the market dictate such standards, or should the government?

The rise of artificial intelligence and robotics will complicate this challenge because, in time, they may make offshoring the manufacture and distribution of goods unnecessary. It may be cheaper and more efficient to bring these operations back to developed countries and use robotic systems instead. What would that mean for local cultures and their economies? In Nike's case, automation is already a concern, particularly as competition from its German rival, Adidas, heats up again.

In considering the ethical challenges presented by the outsourcing of production to lower costs and increase profits, let us return to the example of IBM. IBM has a responsibility to provide technology products of high quality at affordable prices in line with its beliefs about client success, innovation, and trust. If it achieved these ends in a fraudulent or otherwise illegal way, it would be acting irresponsibly and in violation of both US and host country laws and as well as the company's own code of ethics. These constraints appear to leave little room for unethical behavior, yet in a globalized world of intense competition, the temptation to do anything possible to carve out an advantage can be overpowering. This choice between ends and means is reminiscent of the philosophers Aristotle and Kant, both of whom believed it impossible to achieve just ends through unjust means.

But what about consumer responsibility and the impact on the global community? Western consumers tend to perceive globalization as a phenomenon intended to benefit them specifically. In general, they have few compunctions about Western businesses offshoring their manufacturing operations as long as it ultimately benefits them as consumers. However, even in business, ethics is not about consumption but rather about human morality, a greater end. Considering an expansion of domestic markets, what feature of this process enables us to become more humane rather than simply pickier consumers or wasteful spenders? It is the opportunity to encounter other cultures and people, increasing our ethical awareness and sensitivity. Seen in this way, globalization affects the human condition. It raises no less a question than what kind of world we want to leave to our children and grandchildren.

Summary

Culture has a tremendous influence on ethics and its application in a business setting. In fact, we can argue that culture and ethics cannot be separated, because ethical norms have been established over time by and make sense to people who share the same background, language, and customs. For its part, business operates within at least two cultures: its organizational culture and the wider culture in which it was founded. When a business attempts to establish itself in a new environment, a third culture comes into play. With increasingly diverse domestic and global markets and the spread of consumerism, companies must consider the ethical implications of outsourcing production and resist the temptation to look the other way when their values are challenged by the reality of overseas supply or distribution chains.

Offshore Manufacturing Helps Alleviate Poverty in Developing Countries

Ana Revenga and Anabel Gonzalez

Ana Revenga works as a senior fellow at the Brookings Institution. Anabel Gonzalez is the former senior director of the World Bank Group Global Practice on Trade and Competitiveness.

In the ongoing debate about the benefits of trade, we must not lose sight of a vital fact. Trade and global integration have raised incomes across the world, while dramatically cutting poverty *and* global inequality.

Within some countries, trade has contributed to rising inequality, but that unfortunate result ultimately reflects the need for stronger safety nets and better social and labor programs, not trade protection.

Merchandise trade as a share of world GDP grew from around 30 percent in 1988 to around 50 percent in 2013. In this period of rapid globalization, average income grew by 24 percent globally, the global poverty headcount ratio declined from 35% to 10.7%, and the income of the bottom 40 percent of the world population increased by close to 50 percent.

This big picture evidence is buttressed by compelling microeconometric studies on pro-poor income and consumption gains.

- The 2001, US-Vietnam free trade agreement reduced poverty in Vietnam by increasing wage premiums in export sectors, spurring job reallocation from agriculture, forestry and fishing into manufacturing, and stimulating enterprise job growth.
- A study of 27 industrial and 13 developing countries finds that shutting off trade would deprive the richest 10 percent of 28 percent of their purchasing power, but the poorest 10 percent would lose 63 percent because they buy relatively more imported goods.

"Trade has been a global force for less poverty and higher incomes," by Ana Revenga and Anabel Gonzalez, The World Bank Group, February 2, 2017. Reprinted by permission.

- In many developing countries, export growth has been associated with greater gender equality. Exporting firms generally employ a significantly higher share of women than non-exporters. In Cambodia's export-oriented garment sector, which is one of the main providers of wage employment in Cambodia, 85 percent of all workers are women.

A retreat from global integration would erode these gains, especially in developing countries. For example, abandoning existing agreements in the Americas would have particularly large negative welfare effects in countries like Mexico (4 to 9 percent), El Salvador (2 to 5 percent), and Honduras (2 to 5 percent), according to early research at the World Bank.

Within countries there are invariably losers as well as winners from trade and globalization. Households are likely to be affected differently depending on their physical and human capital endowments, their consumption patterns, and their incomes. Among developing countries, which we study most closely at the World Bank, there are countries where the direct effect of trade on the wage distribution has been equalizing (e.g. Brazil), and others where it has been un-equalizing (e.g. Mexico). Trade also reduced the (relative) wages of the poor in India in the 1990s, so that poverty decreased less in rural districts more exposed to trade liberalization.

Work-in-progress by some of our colleagues in the World Bank's Research Group seeks to quantify the potential tradeoff between the efficiency gains and inequality costs of trade liberalization using household survey data from 53 low and middle income countries (Artuc, Porto and Rijkers, "Trading-off the Income Gains and the Inequality Costs of Trade Policy," mimeo: World Bank, 2017, in progress). In spite of heterogeneity in the distributional impacts, hard trade-offs are found only in a relatively small number of countries (such as Burundi, Nigeria and Gambia). In the vast majority of countries (including Egypt, Pakistan, and South Africa) trade liberalization significantly raises incomes with at most trivial inequality costs.

Despite the potentially negative effects of trade on some, what happens to final incomes and hence to inequality, however, is not a given. Between 1990 and 2010, a period of rapid globalization, inequality (measured by the Gini index) increased in the United States from 43 to 47 but fell in Denmark from 31 to 26.

Consider why. US workers concentrated in communities which face high volumes of Chinese imports have experienced fewer jobs and falling wages. And yet, the US Trade Adjustment Assistance (TAA) program falls short of the challenge of helping people get back on their feet. The US spends just 0.1% of GDP on all its active labor market polices while the OECD average is 0.6%. Second, the TAA is designed to help only workers suffering direct trade-related job losses but wages losses are not limited to workers who are employed in import competing sectors. Third, the TAA requires active participation of eligible workers in retraining programs but many less educated and older workers, who are worst affected, fail to qualify because they have often already withdrawn from the labor force.

In Denmark, trade liberalization and offshoring also contributed to a decrease in low skill wages, and increase in high skill wages, thus potentially widening inequality. However, the Danish labor assistance system (called Flexicurity) may have helped to avoid any significant increase in inequality. The system targets all workers suffering from job losses, not just workers in sectors exposed to trade and offshoring shocks, and deals with any negative labor market shock, not just relating to trade. The system is based on: a flexible labor market allowing employers to hire and fire relatively easily; a generous unemployment benefit system; and strong activation policies encouraging job search and enhancing workers' employability.

In countries where trade has created losers, policies that redistribute some of the gains from winners to losers are needed to ensure the benefits of trade are widely shared. They also need policies to better equip workers to benefit from the opportunities offered by trade. Better and more generous safety nets and other social protection policies, and more investments in skill acquisition, are the answer. Not protectionist trade policies that will blunt the engine of growth that has delivered prosperity for millions around the world. This insight guides our work in a World Bank Group dedicated to ending extreme poverty and boosting shared prosperity for all.

Despite Their Reputation, Sweatshops Are Essential to Developing Economies

Prachi Juneja

Prachi Juneja is an author with the Management Study Guide. The Management Study Guide was founded in 2008 and serves as a portal to help students and professionals access an expanded list of guides on different management-related topics.

The term "sweatshops" has been used a lot by the American media or the media in developed nations at large. The sweatshops refer to subcontracting arrangements that big multinational firms like Nike and Adidas have with subcontractors in third world countries like Bangladesh. The provisions are made to exploit the low cost of labor present in these countries.

The argument made by people against sweatshops is that the working conditions there are horrific and instead of providing employment, they are actually causing mayhem. Since the multi-nationals themselves do not perform most of the work, there is no reliable data available for these sweatshops. Many feel that this is actually a conspiracy by the multi-nationals who do not want to perform the dirty tasks themselves but would rather outsource it to contractors.

This article argues that the so-called miserable working conditions are the best alternative for the workers. In a world where every social group and every person are influenced to feel sweatshops are bad, this article will take a contrarian viewpoint.

What Exactly Are Sweatshops?

Sweatshop is a vague term and does not have any precise meaning. The meaning inferred by most is that sweatshops provide very

"The Argument for Sweatshops," by Prachi Juneja, Management Study Guide. Retrieved from https://www.managementstudyguide.com/argument-for-sweatshops.htm. Reprinted by permission.

low wages to their worker. These wages are not even enough to sustain a normal living with one job. Also, there is no job security at these sweatshops. The working conditions are deplorable, and in some cases, they are hazardous i.e. cause occupational illnesses in the long term. A lot of these sweatshops possibly involve child labor as well.

The definitions are vague, and no one can provide precise numbers as to what constitutes a sweatshop. In fact in most sweatshops wages are bad by western standards, but they are very good by local standards. Long hours and poor working conditions seem to be a constant reality everywhere.

The Demands Against Sweatshops

Social groups are demanding that sweatshops should be considered as extensions of the multinationals themselves. As a result, they want these sweatshops to be held to the standard of western laws. This would mean a huge increase in the wages paid out to these sweatshop workers. Also, the cost of employment will rise if the hours are cut, and working conditions are improved. All this will lead to an increase in the cost of production for multi-national companies. Another demand to prevent employment of child labor is the only one that seems to be legitimate.

How Are Wages Set?

Merely imposing laws does not increase wages. In fact, in a globalized world, the imposition of such rules leads to movement of jobs to other countries. To increase jobs, the productivity of the worker will have to be increased. The other alternative would be to make better opportunities available so that employers pay higher wages in competition. Forceful increment in wages often has detrimental consequences.

The Ulterior Motives for Lobbying

It is no surprise that most of the lobbying against sweatshops is being done by social groups in developed countries. They have an ulterior motive and are funded by unions. If the wages are raised in sweatshops, the workers will become more expensive there. As a result, it would make sense to move jobs back home and pay the higher wages to the local population itself. The apparent benevolence is an attempt to price the other workers out of the market.

Much Worse Outcomes

Imposition of laws proposed by the social groups would lead to worse consequences.

- **Minimum Wage Causes Automation:** A higher minimum wage would create a case for automation. This has happened in the United States and will happen in the third world countries as well. Most low wage jobs performed in sweatshops are also low skilled jobs. These jobs are easy to automate and the only thing preventing this automation is the low cost of paying these workers.
- **Minimum Wage Creates Higher Skilled Jobs:** As automation takes places, low skilled jobs change into high skilled jobs. Sweepers are replaced by technicians who can repair vacuum cleaners. As a result, sweatshops will no longer be required. The countries that have these sweatshops do not have any high skilled laborers. By raising the cost of low-skilled laborers, a demand of higher skilled workers will be created and multinationals will be forced to head back home to fulfill this demand.
- **Minimum Wages Causes Migration to Agriculture:** Sweatshops may seem like a bad alternative to the western laborer. However, in countries like Bangladesh and Thailand where they exist, sweatshops are relatively high paying jobs. If they were not so, it would make no sense for the workers in these arrangements to quit their farm jobs, migrate to cities and survive in deplorable living and working conditions to work on this job.

  The reality is that the alternative to these jobs is even worse than sweatshops. Agricultural labor in most of these countries involves more hard labor and pays far less money. The exploitation by multinationals is no comparison to the hardships that these workers will have to face when they work with local landowners.

To sum it up, sweatshops are not a menace at all! In fact, they may look ugly to Westerners but are an important source of employment for the people that work in them. Raising wages and working conditions will create a condition that will lead these sweatshops to shut down and will leave the workers worse off.

Lifting People Out of Poverty Is the Greatest Benefit of Foreign Manufacturing

Marc Gunther

Marc Gunther is a journalist for the Guardian *who writes about business and sustainability. He currently works as an editor-at-large for the* Guardian Sustainable Business US *weekly newsletter.*

So much attention is paid to deplorable factory conditions in poor countries that it's easy to forget that global supply chains for electronics, apparel and toys have helped lift masses of people out of poverty. Since 1980, 680 million people have risen out of poverty in China which has seen its extreme-poverty rate fall from 84% to about 10%, largely because of trade, reports The Economist.

Now, a small number of companies, nonprofits and foundations want to see if the rapidly growing global supply chains that process data and operate call centers—an industry usually described as business processing outsourcing, or BPO—can be deployed to help alleviate poverty in Africa and South Asia. Can outsourcing, a business driven by the search for cheap labor, reconfigure itself to do good?

"By responsibly and ethically employing hundreds of thousands of people, BPOs have a role to play in shifting the social landscape in emerging economies around the world," says a report called Outsourcing for Social Good from Telus International, a Canadian outsourcing firm, and Impakt, a social responsibility consultancy.

Others agree. The Rockefeller Foundation has committed $100m to a project called Digital Jobs Africa that aims to improve one million lives in six African nations. A nonprofit called Samasource organizes poor women and youth in Africa and Asia to deliver data services to such businesses as Microsoft and Google. And a company called Cloud Factory that operates in

"Using outsourcing to help alleviate poverty in Africa and South Asia," by Marc Gunther, Guardian News and Media Limited, June 19, 2014. Reprinted by permission.

Kenya and Nepal says digital outsourcing can "flatten the world, connect people into the global economy and raise up leaders to fight poverty and change their communities."

The pioneer of what is called socially-responsible outsourcing or simply impact sourcing is DDD (Digital Divide Data), a New York-based nonprofit that operates for-profit data centers in Cambodia, Laos and Kenya. DDD and its impact-oriented peers set themselves apart from outsourcing giants such as Tata, Accenture and Infosys because, they say, they deliberately seek out workers in the some of the world's poorest places and provide them not just with jobs, but with the education, training and career counseling they need to rise into the middle class.

"Our ultimate mission is to alleviate poverty," says Jeremy Hockenstein, 42, the founder and CEO of DDD. "We focus on students who are finishing high school, who are very motivated and very smart and who come from low-income homes."

DDD got started in 2001 when Hockenstein, who was then a consultant for McKinsey, was on assignment in Asia and visited Cambodia. "I saw a lot of people learning computers and English, and I didn't see a lot of opportunities," he said. Figuring he had the connections to find them work, he formed DDD and secured as its first client the Harvard Crimson, which had digitized its 20th century archives but wanted to do the same with newspapers published between 1873 and 1899. "It turned out that the socially redeeming value of a crew race between Harvard and Yale (back then) was that it created a job in Cambodia 110 years later," jokes Hockenstein, a Harvard grad. DDD went on to work for campus newspapers and libraries at Yale and Tufts.

Not until 2007 did Hockenstein devote himself full-time to DDD. Since then, the firm has grown briskly and hired senior executives from big outsourcing companies. The company now employs about 500 people in Cambodia, 250 in Laos and 450 in Nairobi, Kenya, its fastest growing operation. Its clients include the British Library, the online genealogy firm ancestry.com and the watchmaker Fossil.

The firm also has close ties to Silicon Valley. The Stanford University library and Google have been both clients, and Michael Chertok, DDD's chief development officer, is a Stanford MBA who worked for Global Catalyst Partners, a venture capital firm that was an early donor to DDD. Cisco and the Skoll Foundation have also supported DDD.

Currently, DDD's client revenues cover its operational costs, and donations pay for training and college scholarships. The company hopes to be self-sustaining as it grows, but its goal is also to become a model for the big outsourcing firms. As Chertok says: "We're not going to be employing millions, and the scale of the problem requires employing millions."

Market dynamics will help. Already, one reason why impact sourcing firms such as DDD can compete with the BPO giants is that labor costs are rising in India and the Philippines, the two English-speaking countries where the BPO industry is strongest. The Telus report also predicts the reputation-conscious brands will ask for more socially-responsible behavior from outsourcing firms, just as they have from their other suppliers. Like DDD and Samasource, Telus now helps some of its workers to earn college degrees. "When people feel valued and cared for, they become more loyal and enthusiastic about the organization they are working for," the report says. That kind of thinking could turn the reputation of outsourcing around.

Sweatshops Use Cheap Labor and Place Local Workers in Inhumane Conditions

Jason Hickel

Jason Hickel is a professor and anthropologist who has written for the Guardian, Al Jazeera, *the* Financial Times, *and* Foreign Policy.

The news that a Romanian sweatshop manufactured one of Kate Middleton's most famous dresses has inspired renewed popular interest in the ethics and economics of outsourcing jobs to utilize super-cheap labor. This is only the most recent of a string of cases that exemplify the shocking proliferation of sweatshops—even across Europe—over the past few decades. But the truly troubling part of the story is the logic that Kate's defenders have invoked to justify this trend, drawing on arguments made by allegedly "progressive" US economists.

Jeffrey Sachs, well-known author of *The End of Poverty,* once famously stated, "My concern is not that there are too many sweatshops, but that there are too few." Similarly Paul Krugman has argued that sweatshops "move hundreds of millions of people from abject poverty to something still awful but nonetheless significantly better… [so] the growth of sweatshop employment is tremendous good news for the world's poor."

In a *New York Times Magazine* article disturbingly titled "Two Cheers for Sweatshops," Nicholas Kristof endorsed this logic by explaining that when he first moved to Asia he, "like most Westerners," was outraged at the sweatshops, but eventually came to appreciate them as "a clear sign of the industrial revolution that is beginning to reshape Asia." He pointed out that "Asian workers would be aghast at the idea of American consumers boycotting

"Rethinking Sweatshop Economics," by Jason Hickel, Foreign Policy In Focus, July 1, 2011, https://fpif.org/rethinking_sweatshop_economics/. Licensed under CC BY-ND 3.0 International.

certain toys or clothing in protest. The simplest way to help the poorest Asians would be to buy more from sweatshops, not less."

These arguments all turn on one simple idea that often vanquishes critics with its apparently unassailable economic logic: that sweatshops exist because people are willing to take sweatshop jobs at sweatshop wages. People have a choice in where they go to work, the thinking goes, and sweatshops are often the best deal in town—certainly better than no job at all. If sweatshops didn't exist, then millions of people would be hungry on the streets.

This view rests on the assumption that countries that attract sweatshops have always been populated with masses of poor people desperate for wages, that poverty is somehow an *a priori* condition. In such a world, sweatshops can only be a boon.

But this assumption entirely misses the crucial point about poverty. People—in Thailand and Peru, for example—only choose sweatshop jobs because they have been *made* desperate and given no alternatives for livelihood. So it's not really a "choice" at all. They are forced by circumstance to sell themselves into sub-human conditions. Sociologists refer to this as the "structural violence" of unemployment.

Colonial and Neoliberal Legacies

The desperation that drives people into sweatshops is a historically recent phenomenon. Most of the people in the so-called third world used to be subsistence farmers who were able to support themselves sufficiently on the yields of their land. That started to change under late-19th-century colonial regimes. In most places in Africa, Asia, and South America, colonizers initially had a very difficult time getting natives to work in their mines, factories, and plantations. To solve this problem, they either forcibly removed farmers from their land or levied onerous taxes in order to coerce them into seeking wage work, all under the guise of the "civilizing mission." This caused hundreds of thousands of people to move to industrial cities where they constituted a reserve army of workers willing to take whatever job they could find and ready to underbid each others' wages.

In the colonial context, substandard wages were not the neutral product of market efficiency but the outcome of a deliberate strategy to render people desperate enough to take jobs that paid pennies. But only recently did things get bad enough that sweatshops started springing up. Beginning in the late 1970s, the World Bank, the International Monetary Fund, and later the World Trade Organization began pushing new forms of market deregulation—known as "structural adjustment programs"—on third world governments, requiring them to stop subsidizing their agricultural sectors and to allow cheap imported grains into their markets. These neoliberal policies crippled small-scale farming to the point of collapse and created a second wave of people forced to migrate to cities to survive.

This happened at the same time as two other crucial structural adjustments. First, protective trade tariffs were drastically reduced, allowing Western corporations to move their operations offshore without paying prohibitive import duties. Second, important labor regulations like collective bargaining rights and high minimum wages were curbed or cut, to the point of giving corporations the power to sue their host governments for regulations that diminish returns on investment. This created an ideal environment for companies like Nike, Walmart, and General Motors to move their production facilities to places where they get away with paying workers many times less than developed economies would ever allow. This process of seeking the most exploitable location possible has become known as "the race to the bottom"—the dark underbelly of what economists so calmly encourage as "comparative advantage."

A 2002 study conducted by economist Robert Pollin found that the retail prices of clothing in the United States would have to rise by only 1.8 percent in order to cover a 100 percent wage increase for sweatshop workers in Mexican garment factories. In other words, the price of Kate's £175 dress would increase to

£178.15, with the additional money doubling the wages of the seamstresses who made it. This is especially important in light of a 1999 study by the National Bureau of Economic Research that found that consumers were willing to pay 15 percent more on a $100 item—and 28 percent more on a $10 item—if it was made under "good working conditions."

The point here is that companies do not *have* to use sweatshop labor to earn profits, just as workers in third world countries do not *have* to be desperate enough to work in sweatshops. None of this is natural or inevitable, despite what sweatshop enthusiasts are so eager to have us believe. Sachs' and Krugman's absurd conclusion that we should promote sweatshops as a solution to the problem of global poverty derives from a profound deficit of historical perspective. It is a shame that the most cherished priests of progressive economics have nothing to offer beyond a world of sweatshops justified beneath the banner of "market freedom" and comparative advantage. That this has become the utopian vision of our time is tragic.

A New Economics

A few targeted changes to global trade rules could create a world where sweatshops don't have to exist. If developing countries were allowed to erect import tariffs to protect small-scale agriculture and enforce labor regulations to ensure that every working citizen earned a living wage, the sweatshop concept would be completely unnecessary. Of course, if the workers that make shoes, clothes, and electronics for Western consumers were earning decent wages, that would mean that we would all pay a little bit more for our stuff, and the companies that make it might net a little bit less. But income redistribution along these lines would hardly be a bad thing, especially given today's historically unprecedented levels of social inequality: The wealthiest one percent of the world's population controls 40 percent of the world's wealth while the bottom 50 percent controls a mere one percent.

The counter-argument holds that if working conditions become too humane and wages too decent in any given country companies will relocate to more welcoming states, hurting GDP and leaving the poor with fewer employment opportunities. This could be solved with an international minimum wage law (putting a floor on the race to the bottom) and a targeted trade quota system that channels foreign direct investment to where it is needed to alleviate poverty rather than to where labor is most exploitable. In addition, states can help create good jobs for their citizens by protecting local infant industries and by implementing import substitution programs.

Such policies have been tried before. The United States, Great Britain, and virtually every major economic power have been built on precisely these principles, and they were standard practice for many developing countries emerging from colonialism in the 1960s. If the developing world were to reinstate these policies—winding back the clock to a time before structural adjustment—they would be able to significantly improve local employment and generate an additional $480 billion per year in GDP above current levels. But such reforms would require confronting the entrenched interests of the states and corporations that control global trade policy for their own narrow benefit.

Sweatshops may indeed be preferable to poverty. But instead of taking poverty for granted in the first place, we should question the processes that produce it—the policies that make people desperate. Sweatshops are an easy, unthinking solution, and only make sense if we are ready to bend to the dictates of "market efficiency" and accept exploitation as economically rational. What we need is a new economics, one that can think beyond the limited boundaries of neoliberal ideology and make an effort to construct a more humane and democratic world. The question is not whether we have the ability to do this, but whether we have the courage.

Beyond the Cheap Labor, Sweatshops Have a Human Cost

Rebecca Prentice and Geert De Neve

Rebecca Prentice serves as a senior lecturer of anthropology at the University of Sussex in the United Kingdom. Geert De Neve is a professor of social anthropology and South Asian studies at the University of Sussex.

Exactly five years ago, in November 2012, a fire in the Tazreen Fashions factory in Bangladesh killed at least 112 workers. Probably caused by a short circuit on the ground floor of the building, the fire rapidly spread up the nine floors where garment workers were trapped due to narrow or blocked fire escapes. Many died inside the building or while seeking an escape through the windows.

Just five months later, the collapse of the Rana Plaza building killed 1,134 garment workers and injured hundreds of survivors. Rana Plaza was an eight-storey commercial building that housed garment units on its upper levels. The building that collapsed had already been evacuated the day before after cracks were identified, but the factory management had made workers return to work under the pressure of looming shipping deadlines. During the morning rush hour, the building collapsed in on itself like a house of cards.

These two incidents and a string of other disasters in garment factories across South Asia exposed the brutal employment conditions in the garment industry, and the deadly cost of "fast fashion" to workers who produce clothes under strict deadlines for very low wages. In the ensuing years, a number of new initiatives

"Five years after deadly factory fire, Bangladesh's garment workers are still vulnerable," by Rebecca Prentice and Geert De Neve, The Conversation, November 23, 2017. https://theconversation.com/five-years-after-deadly-factory-fire-bangladeshs-garment-workers-are-still-vulnerable-88027. Licensed under CC BY-ND 4.0 International.

have been set up to improve factory safety and compensate injured workers and the families of those killed.

The 2013 Accord on Fire and Building Safety in Bangladesh, a safety pact signed by global unions and more than 200 brands, has taken important steps towards making global apparel companies accountable for the safety of factories in their supply chains. Measures taken include a series of building inspections, upgrades and closures where buildings are deemed structurally unsafe, as well as an attempt at making brands and retailers contractually liable for the safety of the factories where their garments are produced.

But five years on, not enough is being done to protect garment workers, and these new initiatives haven't gone far enough to address the multiple attacks on workers' everyday health and well-being.

Codes of conduct, continually used by apparel companies to monitor the working conditions of their suppliers, narrowly focus on building safety and physical infrastructure with a bias towards what can be seen and audited. These codes are poorly implemented, allowing building fires and collapses to continue; they also ignore many things that threaten workers' health and well-being on a day-to-day basis.

The Accord on Fire and Building Safety in Bangladesh likewise focuses exclusively on physical infrastructure, leaving out a host of other issues that affect workers' health on a daily basis and undermine their long-term well-being: long working hours, physical and bodily exhaustion, intense work rhythms, harassment, and the lack of any meaningful representation. All these problems and more are still too often invisible.

Everyday Risks

In our new book, *Unmaking the Global Sweatshop: Health and Safety of the World's Garment Workers*, Hasan Ashraf, a Bangladeshi anthropologist who conducted six months of fieldwork at a Dhaka knitwear factory, writes about the long list of everyday health threats he witnessed: everything from dust and smoke inhalation, noise, lack of ventilation, eyestrain, musculoskeletal pain, stress, and exposure to lights, electric wires, and chemical adhesives. Ashraf discovered that workers are having to make a trade-off between earning a living and caring for their health, which can rapidly depreciate during their working lives, undermining their long-term physical and mental well-being.

Similarly, a recent report by the non-profit organisation Better Factories Cambodia also concluded that poor working conditions "have contributed to a wave of incidents of mass fainting among Cambodian factory workers—allegedly caused, at least in part, by exhaustion, overheating, and malnutrition."

The fast fashion industry needs to realise that for garment workers, health means more than just the absence of injury. It encompasses physical, social, and mental health, all of which are threatened by the stress and stigma that extend well beyond the shop floor and into workers' lives long after they stop working.

Everyone and every organisation involved in the global clothing supply chain needs to consider not only the symptoms of ill health, but also its causes. And one of the central causes is the global system of the industry itself, which relies on outsourcing and subcontracting and offloads the social costs and risks of garment production onto already vulnerable workers in countries such as Bangladesh and Cambodia.

The future well-being of garment workers around the world relies on the industry accepting its responsibility to these people—and understanding that that responsibility extends well beyond the structural safety of the buildings they work in.

Offshore Manufacturing Promotes Child Labor and Unsustainable Wages

Simon Parry

Simon Parry writes for the South China Morning Post. *He has recently covered the civil unrest in Hong Kong.*

I n a suite of offices lined with racks of clothes on the seventh floor of an industrial building in the back streets of Lai Chi Kok, the head of a trading company explains the economic reality that has transformed the global garment industry over the past decade.

"Ten years ago, you could only buy a T-shirt for US$5. Now you can buy a sweater for US$6, and for US$9 you can buy a jacket," says Mandarin Lui Wing-har, managing director of the low-profile but highly influential Top Grade International Enterprise. "Of course, at the high end of the market, people will still pay US$500 for a T-shirt. They don't care about the price, only the brand, and maybe only 50 T-shirts will be made in that style. But we are making maybe 50,000 T-shirts in each style—and that is why we can sell them for US$3 or US$4."

A decade ago, most of those T-shirts would have been made in Guangdong, a province once known as the "world's workshop." Today, the looms are turning faster than ever—but the work has moved nearly 2,500km from Dongguan to Dhaka. Soaring labour costs and China's gradual shift from low-end to high-end manufacturing have seen garment production find a new home in Bangladesh. But the doorway to the world's workshop remains in Hong Kong.

In the same way Kowloon-based companies would send mainland-made products around the world throughout the 1990s and 2000s, Top Grade last year handled orders for 30 million pieces

"The true cost of your cheap clothes: slave wages for Bangladesh factory workers," by Simon Parry, South China Morning Post Publishers Ltd, June 11, 2016. Reprinted by permission.

of clothing made in Dhaka's factories for customers including European supermarket chain Lidl, and major chains in Brazil and Japan. Orders are placed with Top Grade and other companies, such as Li & Fung, and the payments pass through their Hong Kong offices, although the goods themselves are sent from Bangladesh directly to the customer.

As clothing factories in southern China close down, Top Grade is seeing orders boom. The company had the prescience to set up in Bangladesh before most of its competitors and now has 20 to 30 factories in Dhaka. Lui and her industry colleagues expect Bangladesh to overtake the mainland as the world's biggest garment producer in a matter of years.

More than four million people work in Bangladesh's garment industry, which now accounts for about 80 per cent of the country's foreign trade. It has the potential to lift the nation out of poverty in the same way manufacturing transformed the lives of tens of millions of migrant workers in China in the 1980s and 90s. But the relentless demand for ever-cheaper clothes from high-street stores and supermarket chains in the West is keeping workers' wages at levels as low as US$68 a month—an amount that pressure groups, unions and even some employers admit is barely enough to support the people whose sweat and hard work the industry relies on.

The Rana Plaza disaster in 2013, in which 1,130 people died and 2,500 were injured when a run-down eight-storey factory complex making clothes for Primark, Benetton, Walmart and other Western brands collapsed, highlighted the dangers of the industry in Bangladesh. Critics say that while fire and building safety conditions have improved since the tragedy, worker conditions remain bleak, particularly as the pressure increases on factories to produce ever cheaper clothes.

"Since the disaster, employees have to work harder," says former child factory worker Nazma Akter, founder of the 37,000-member Awaj Foundation, which fights for labour rights in Bangladesh. "They have higher production targets. If they cannot fulfil them they have to work extra hours but with no overtime. It is very tough; they cannot go for toilet breaks or to drink water. They become sick. They are getting the minimum wage as per legal requirements but they are not getting a living wage."

A survey of Bangladeshi factories supplying Marks & Spencer carried out last summer found that workers' average basic monthly pay was 6,500 taka (HK$630) and their average take-home pay, including an average two hours a day of overtime, was 8,000 taka. Although this is more than many in the industry get, the average estimate of what workers consider is enough to live on and support their families is 15,000 taka a month—about twice their actual pay.

Workers in Bangladesh have some of the lowest salaries anywhere in the world.

"Even Myanmar is getting US$99," Akter points out. "Our workers need a monthly rise of US$30 or more."

Akter criticises the use of foreign aid, which poured into Bangladesh after the Rana Plaza disaster from governments and Western companies making clothes in the country.

"If this money went to individual workers, they would have a more happy life. But the money was invested elsewhere. Workplace education is important but we need to address the fact that workers are not getting sufficient food and have no freedom of association."

Women in the garment industry come to Dhaka from the countryside. "After they reach 40 or 45 they voluntarily leave their jobs because they become old and they cannot fulfil their production targets any longer," Akter says. "There is too much work pressure and they have not enough food and they suffer malnutrition. They spend most of their youth in the garment industry for multinational retailers and then they have to retire at 40, when their health is ruined.

"H&M, Primark, Asda, Tesco, M&S—they come here [many of the brands buy direct through their own offices in Dhaka, but may also employ third parties such as Top Grade] because Bangladesh is cheap and they get cheap labour. It is not fair. Humans cannot be so cheap. There needs to be a balance—you cannot say you are trying to improve working conditions and help workers out on one hand when on the other hand you are not giving a fair price," she says.

"Consumers in [the West] have a big responsibility. They get things so cheap. They have to think about how these companies are doing business. The multinationals take our blood and our sweat. Consumers need to know where their clothes are coming from and what the working hours and conditions are. We need to look at the living conditions, not the working conditions."

Akter's call for fairer prices is echoed by Dhaka factory owner Emdadul Islam, director of the Babylon Group, which employs more than 10,000 workers to make clothes for companies such as Tesco and River Island.

"When companies do business with suppliers like us they should be able to understand the right kind of price for the articles they buy," he says. "Sometimes they seem to be void of any sense of that. They don't give a damn if it is a rational price or not. They say, 'I can get it cheaper next door so you should be even cheaper.' When you talk about your cost or margins they say, 'This is something I don't deal with. I have my target.' When you raise ethical social issues, it is a one-sided conversation."

Workers are getting too little, Islam concedes, but adds, "It is difficult for factories like us … because we are not being compensated properly in terms of the price we get from buyers and customers.

"We need to avoid a repetition of the Rana Plaza incident. For that to happen, these suppliers need to be able to sell their products at the right prices. How can it be a cheaper price every day? Where is the magic that makes that happen? If you exploit your suppliers every day, at some point you cross the line and you are no longer an ethical buyer."

Islam suggests a US$1 levy on every US$20 item of clothing that would go directly to workers.

"In the past, you simply could not guarantee this extra money would benefit the workers. But today it is different. It is time they did it," he says.

But at Bangladeshi conglomerate Viyellatex, which employs 18,000 people and makes clothes for several high-street chains, chief operating officer Ziauddin Ahmed disagrees with the proposal and says there has been too much focus on the pay of garment workers.

"What about rickshaw operators or street vendors? What about the people working in street restaurants? They are all human beings too," he says. "As a responsible manufacturer we comply with government rules [on minimum pay]. Of course, we would like all our workers to come into work driving a fantastic car. But would you be able to buy the T-shirt then? If you go to London, you will see people smuggled in from other countries and working in the restaurants and kitchens and not getting the legal requirements. Things like this happen everywhere but everyone points the finger at us."

The responsibility lies with consumers, says Ahmed.

"You are supporting the culture of cheap products. If you have an order for a million T-shirts and we can't meet the price, the buyer will go to a noncompliant factory because they will do it very cheaply. If people start to think, 'I don't only need to buy cheaply but I need to buy responsibly,' that is when things will start to change. When customers say, 'I will only buy a sustainable product that has been made responsibly,' the entire supply chain will change, because the market rules. It is the customer who is the king."

At British-based pressure group Labour Behind the Label, policy director Anna McMullen says governments need to demand more data on the source of imported garments to stop worker abuse.

"The cost of cheap clothes is people living in poverty and factories cutting corners on health and safety, and that's not right," she says. "We can ask companies to put a label on their clothing saying this is the factory where it was made. That way, we get civil society engaging in where our clothes come from and who really made this."

Reports about poor working conditions and suggestions about how to improve them are nothing new, of course, but there is no sign of consumers forcing an improvement in the living standards for garment workers any time soon. If anything, the switch to production in more freewheeling Bangladesh is being accelerated by the global slowdown, which has sharpened shoppers' appetite for bargains.

"Buyers are looking for good quality and good style but they cannot pay high prices," Lui says. "That is why we survive. We are doing mass production at low cost and that is exactly what Bangladesh can do.

"The whole world is in a recession nowadays. Buyers are under pressure. They don't want the shops to be empty of stock but they can't pay higher prices. People go shopping and they expect to buy a pair of jeans for a few dollars so you have to find the things they want at the prices they want."

Top Grade has 100 staff based in Dhaka to pay regular visits to ensure factories are compliant and there are no issues regarding conditions or underage workers, Lui says.

"Before we place an order, our team will inspect the factory and make sure they have the certificates," she says. "In Bangladesh, you can find tip-top modern factories and you can find lousy factories producing garments for very low prices—but if you place an order with them you will never get your shipment out.

"Every season my people analyse which factory is reliable and on time, and that the price and quality are OK. Some factories are very bad and we take them off our list."

For Lui, the main concerns currently are union-led labour unrest and the threat of Muslim extremism spreading after Islamic State-linked incidents in the country.

"I hope the Bangladeshi government will do something to give us more confidence," she says. "The garment business is too important for them."

At Viyellatex, meanwhile, where rows of workers are making piles of bright green children's shorts for Marks & Spencer, Ahmed insists that, despite the challenges and shortfalls, conditions are improving.

He prefers to emphasise the extraordinary growth the country's garment industry has experienced over the past two decades.

"We are already the second biggest apparel exporting country in the world after China. Soon Bangladesh will be No1," he says, with unmistakable pride. "We can clothe the world."

Underage and Overworked

Bilkis Begum was barely 12 years old when she began working in a Dhaka garment factory.

"My parents didn't want me to leave home and come to work here but we had no money," she says. "I was the oldest and I felt responsible. So I came with my uncle to work here."

The daughter of a cycle driver from a village 100km from the Bangladeshi capital, she left school to support her four younger brothers. From 8am to 7pm, she sews shirts and trousers at a factory supplying Western high-street brands. She lives alongside hundreds of other workers in a tin-roofed shack 10 minutes' walk from the factory, on Dhaka's crowded and chaotic outskirts.

"The hours have always been long but as I got older, the work got harder. I was given more and more difficult work," she says.

Under Bangladeshi law, garment factories can only employ workers aged at least 14 and those aged 14 to 18 can work for a maximum of five hours a day.

"When I was younger, every time the inspectors came, I would be ordered to leave the factory or they would hide me and the other underage workers somewhere no one would see us," says Bilkis, who is now 17.

Still earning less than 6,000 taka (HK$580) a month, Bilkis is proud to have been able to support her family for so long.

"My plan is to work until I get married," she says, with a tired smile at the end of another long day's work. "When I get married I don't want to work anymore. I just want to relax and enjoy life."

Offshore Manufacturing Allows Companies to Evade Taxes

Emma Clancy

Emma Clancy is an economist who currently works as an advisor on the economics and tax justice committees in the European Parliament for the European United Left/Nordic Green Left political group.

After the European Commission's state aid ruling on Ireland, both Apple and the Irish government assured us that Apple has paid tax at Ireland's statutory rate of 12.5% since 2014. But our research, following up on the revelations made last November in the Paradise Papers, finds that changes in Ireland's tax law in 2014 have provided Apple with a near-total offset mechanism for sales profits.

Using data from Apple Inc's 10-K filings to the US Securities and Exchange Commission, we estimate that Apple's tax rate for the period 2015-2017 for its non-US earnings is between 3.7% and 6.2%.

Within the EU, Apple paid tax at a rate of between 1.7% and 8.8% during the period 2015-2017. If we assume that Apple's provision for foreign tax is substantially smaller than the amount actually transferred to foreign governments, we estimate that Apple may have paid as little as 0.7% tax in the EU.

Applying this range of estimates, this means that Apple has avoided paying between €4bn-€21bn in tax to EU tax collection agencies during this period.

Ireland remains at the centre of Apple's tax avoidance strategy. Apple organised a new structure in 2014-2015 that included the relocation of its non-US sales and intellectual property (IP) from "nowhere" to Ireland, and the relocation of its overseas cash to Jersey.

"Apple, Ireland and The New Green Jersey Tax Avoidance Technique," by Emma Clancy, Social Europe Publishing & Consulting GmbH, July 4, 2018. Reprinted by permission.

But despite the relocation of sales income and IP assets to Ireland, there was no observable corresponding increase in corporation tax received from Apple by Irish Revenue from 2015-2017.

Industry Designs a Replacement for the Double Irish

The structure Apple uses today was designed by the industry and willingly implemented by the Irish government as a replacement for the Double Irish scheme.

It is based on the use of full capital allowances for expenditure on intellectual property and massive intra-group loans to purchase the IP, with full deductions on the interest paid for these loans, in order to cancel out the tax bill arising from sales profits.

Ireland's capital allowance for intangible assets was introduced in the Finance Act 2009, with a cap of 80%. It meant relief in the form of a capital allowance for expenditure on IP against trading income in a given reporting period or as a write-off against taxable income over 15 years. Deductions for associated interest expenses could also be written off up to an 80% cap.

Our report reveals that the Irish government raised this 80% cap to 100% following lobbying by the American Chamber of Commerce in Ireland in 2014. This resulted in the amount of capital allowances being claimed by multinational corporations rising from €2.7 billion in 2014 to €28.9 billion in 2015.

In 2017 the Irish government announced that it would bring back the 80% cap but said it would not apply to the IP that was brought onshore from 2015-2017, which included Apple's IP assets.

Apple and the "Green Jersey" Technique

Our research indicates that, with the assistance of the Irish government, Apple has successfully created a new structure that allows IP and sales profit to be onshored, but the company is granted a tax write-off against almost all of its non-US sales profits.

Apple is achieving this by using:

- A capital allowance for depreciation of intangible assets at a rate of 100%;
- A massive outflow of capital from its Ireland-based subsidiaries to its Jersey-based subsidiaries in the form of debt from intra-group loans used to fund the IP acquisition;
- Interest deductions of 100% on these intra-group loans;

While several multinationals continue to use the Double Irish, which will not be phased out until 2020, briefings on Ireland's tax regime from offshore law firms suggest this structure is the new normal—a "typical" structure now used by companies that trade in IP.

We call it the "Green Jersey" in reference to the Paradise Papers revelations regarding Apple's use of Jersey in its new structure.

The essential features of this technique are:

- It can be used by large multinational corporations engaged in trading in IP;
- It has specifically been designed by the Irish government to facilitate near-total tax avoidance by the same companies who were using the Double Irish tax avoidance scheme;
- While the Double Irish was characterized by the flow of outbound royalty payments from Ireland to Irish-registered but offshore-tax resident subsidiaries, this scheme is characterized by the onshoring of IP and sales profits to Ireland;
- Sales profits are booked in Ireland, but the expenditure the company incurs in the one-off purchase of the IP license(s) can be written off against the sales profits by using the capital allowance program for intangible assets;
- It is beneficial for the company to complement the tax write-off by continuing to use an offshore subsidiary, but no longer for outbound royalty payments. The role of the offshore subsidiary is to store cash and provide loans to the Irish subsidiary to fund the purchase of the IP. The expenditure on the IP is written off, but so too are the associated interest

payments made to the offshore subsidiary, which thus accumulates more cash that goes untaxed.

The new structure has allowed Apple to almost double the mountain of cash it holds in offshore tax havens, as highlighted by the ICIJ.

The law governing the use of capital allowances for IP is not subject to Ireland's transfer pricing legislation, but it includes a prohibition from being used for tax avoidance purposes. Apple is potentially breaking Irish law by its restructure and its exploitation of the capital allowance regime for tax purposes.

CHAPTER 3

Are the Benefits of Offshore Manufacturing Sustainable in the Long Run?

Overview: Foreign Manufacturing Offers Both Positive and Negative Outcomes

Synthesis Engineering Services

Synthesis is an engineering and design services company that was founded by Eldon Goates. It offers consulting, product design and development, and other engineering services.

It's a dilemma: Should you get the widget made offshore? Or at home? There are a lot of interrelated and complex parts to answering this question, so, how do you choose? We'll talk about a few pros and cons of foreign manufacturing vs. domestic—from the engineer's perspective.

Offshore—Foreign Manufacturing

What we call "Offshore Manufacturing" has less to do with oceans as the phrase implies (though it fits many instances). It is, perhaps, better termed "Foreign Manufacturing" meaning not produced domestically. "Offshoring" is another term for moving processes out of the country. Either way, these mean the country of design origin and intend consumption is different than the country where manufacturing is done.

The trend in the last many years (especially in the USA) is more and more manufacturing in other countries. In public there's talk of keeping things at home, but reality still sees a lot of manufacturing where regulations are lax or labor is cheap. Of course, there are dozens of arguments about whether this is good, but I'll leave that for later.

There are advantages and disadvantages for sure. In our experience with foreign manufacturing, some customers have success and others not so much. What's the difference? Let's look at both with an eye to averting disasters.

"Pros and Cons: Foreign Manufacturing or Domestic?" Synthesis Engineering Services, Inc. Reprinted by permission.

Foreign Manufacturing Decision Points

In general, we get kind of spoiled by purchasing goods from all over the globe. We see things on the internet, and easily buy them even though they come from elsewhere. It comes in a box and we don't think much more about it. What we don't see is the network behind the scenes that makes it happen. When you start manufacturing offshore, you get to manage that network (or hire someone to do it).

In considering the options, here are some things to think about:

- First, foreign manufacturing is never as easy as it appears.
- There are many outside factors in cost—shipping, tariffs, import fees, export fees, government extras, travel, brokers, exchange rates etc...
- Acquiring goods from another country involves help from outside your company—finding reliable partners (for shipping, unraveling government regulations, etc.), timing issues, factory delays, special holidays, . . .

Then the practical side like:

- How well do you speak the language?
- Do you know the trade and business customs?
- Who do you know to guide you?
- Can you find a fair, reliable agent to handle things? If so, what do they charge?
- What resources do you have to assure quality? (And, What happens when you get a container load of widgets that are not right?)
- An unscrupulous factory might make shortcuts in production to save a buck. (Yes, this can happen anywhere, but it seems to happen more when the manufacturing facility is far from the customer. Especially when legal recourse is less likely.)
- How much control do you want over the product? Over quality?

Is this negative? No. Foreign manufacturing adds a layer of complexity, and cost-benefit, is not just money. So, how about some first-hand examples?

Positive Offshore Examples

One of our customers does all of their manufacturing offshore. They have a few select factories in China that produce the bulk of their product—10's of thousands of pieces in dozens of skews. On the whole they are quite successful, but it doesn't go without some hiccups. Their challenges include:

- Scheduling and timing and planning so product is not late for their distribution customers.
- First batch quality issues. (Once details work out, things usually go well.)
- Hidden material changes (when the factory can't get the specific material or decides to save some money on their end without telling the customer). Sometimes the fall-out of these situations is painful and expensive.
- Prototyping and new product delays.

This customer knows they must do all the design, engineering and prototype work at home, then when things are complete, they can show exactly what they need. Then, they know it takes some time to work through first article issues to establish production. After that, manufacturing usually runs smoothly.

This customer has attempted to bring some manufacturing back domestically, but they struggle to hit the needed price points.

Another customer found the quality of the foreign manufacturing parts is better than those produced domestically. Why? This customer took a lot of time selecting the factory. They sent me to visit factories, discuss needs, assess capability, then they chose a factory that has great quality. Timely delivery is sometimes an issue because this customer is small for a factory with many demands.

Ugly Foreign Manufacturing Examples

After design, this customer sent a prototype along with CAD data to the chosen factory. The factory promised parts in 6 weeks, so this customer made promises to their distribution based on that timing. Sure enough, in 6 weeks the first articles arrived, but every one had a big scratch. Since the scratches are deep, and all the same, it was a mystery. The scratch is an "innie", so not a "scratch" in the mold (or it would be an "outie" on the part). Strange. Finally, when looking at photos, we realized the prototype part we sent had this scratch—from a testing mishap. Anyway, the foreign manufacturing facility duplicated the scratch in their mold. Amazing. Unfortunately, it was another 15 weeks before the customer got good parts. Timing for this client created issues by not meeting deliveries.

Another client sourced their product offshore, with mostly good success. Suddenly they started receiving terrible failure reports from the field. Because the failures are a HUGE safety risk, as more reports came, they began to panic. Synthesis was called to help. Working together, as we isolated the problem as a manufacturing issue. We discovered that a supplier to the manufacturer chose to substitute a weaker component—5000# capacity instead of 8000#—disguised as full capacity. Since the machines operate around 7000#, failures are no surprise. The reasons don't matter. In the end, that choice gave a big black eye. In this case, the supplier put lives at risk trying to save a buck, and the receiving manufacturer did not realize or verify the orders. Unfortunately, at Synthesis we've had 2 other customers with similar issues and heard many such stories.

On the Moral Side

Do you have moral values conflicting with the way a potential vendor manufactures? Things like pollution, or child labor, or working conditions? If you do, then you should consider carefully some aspects of foreign manufacturing.

Think about the factory and your city. Would you like to live by it?

Do you have a strong allegiance to your country and decry other companies that send jobs offshore?

Again, from our experience, if quantity is high enough, and you have time and resources to deal with the details, offshore manufacturing can be a real boon. If not, consider how much of a headache you are willing to accept. Basically, learn before you buy. Careful choices on the front will avoid embarrassment or market rejection later when (not if) customers find out about your manufacturing.

Rethinking Decisions

Some companies that were first to push manufacturing offshore are now re-thinking and bringing some back. Labor rates overseas have risen, and quality concerns have caused some rethinking about what goes out, and what stays home. Since this is a big decision, it's not an exercise to learn WHY as it pertains to your new product.

Once you start manufacturing, it's expensive to move production. That is true of starting domestic and moving to foreign manufacturing or the other way. Choose carefully.

Final Thoughts on Where to Manufacture

Is there manufacturing magic in China, Mexico, Indonesia, the USA or any other country? Sometimes it feels that way, but there are wonderful, helpful, honest people in all of these places. As I travel, and I always find great people. (I don't understand most of the stereotypes—yes, other cultures have different customs, but they are people with goals, ambitions and friends just like everywhere else. We're more the same than different. Enough of my soapbox.)

To assist customers, we have done cost comparisons with USA vs. Foreign Manufacturing, and some comparisons come in favor of a domestic manufacturer. Other studies give the edge to an offshore source. There is no magic. However, there are generalities that seem to hold:

- If the product is still tweaking with development or if you expect running changes, keep it close to home.
- When the product has large, consistent volumes over a long time, it's a candidate for foreign manufacturing.
- If the product is time sensitive from order to delivery, especially if timelines are short, think domestic.
- Most successful companies I have worked with, have specific factories doing production, and they go there frequently to maintain a positive relationship.

There are so many variables in choosing, and your situation has its unique factors. As you consider, just note that decisions are not as easy as they first seem. Go in with eyes open and be flexible.

Despite Popular Beliefs, Offshoring Is Only Responsible for 4 Percent of Domestic Layoffs

Charles L. Schultze

Charles L. Schultze previously worked as a senior fellow emeritus in the economic studies program at the Brookings Institution. He published this viewpoint during his tenure there.

Until the end of 2003, the United States had been experiencing a "jobless" recovery, with employment stagnating at levels well below those in 2000. A widespread perception has arisen that a major culprit behind the dearth of jobs was the growing practice of US firms to relocate part of their domestic operations to lower-wage countries abroad. "Offshoring" presumably caused a reduction in US output and a corresponding loss of jobs.

In fact, after the 2001 recession, US domestic production rose substantially, but output per worker—productivity—jumped so sharply that instead of rising, employment declined. That is the real cause of the jobless recovery. Had GDP growth been accompanied by a continuation of earlier rates of productivity growth, there would have been some 2 million more private sector jobs than there were at the end of 2003.

When firms send work overseas, those goods or services come back in the form of imports. But a careful look at US import data—especially for service imports, where most offshoring growth occurred—indicates that while the total number of jobs affected by offshoring had increased, that number was still small relative to the millions of jobs affected by the productivity surprise.

What Is Offshoring?

There is no official definition of the term "offshoring," but it has come to mean the actions of American firms in relocating some

"Offshoring, Import Competition, and the Jobless Recovery," by Charles L. Schultze, The Brookings Institution, August 1, 2004. Reprinted by permission.

part of their domestic operations to a foreign country, including, for example, automobile firms switching purchases of auto parts from domestic plants to Mexico; computer or software firms transferring some of their programming operations to India; or financial firms relocating major parts of their record-keeping activities to one of the Caribbean countries.

In some cases firms locate overseas operations in foreign affiliates they own and control. Some fraction of the value of the firm's domestic sales now consists of intermediate goods or services imported from those affiliates. The Department of Commerce's Bureau of Economic Analysis (BEA) includes these intra-firm imports in its compilation of US domestic and international economic accounts.

Overseas relocation need not, and very often does not, involve transactions with foreign subsidiaries. Firms can effectively relocate activities abroad by contracting for the purchase of goods and services from independent foreign firms. Nike, for example, has set up an extensive network of independent foreign producers under contract to produce goods for Nike's distribution channels in the United States. There are American and foreign firms who can act as intermediaries to arrange the production of goods and services abroad to meet the needs of smaller American firms that wish to outsource some part of their operations abroad.

While the advent of cheap, high quality, and virtually instantaneous information and communication facilities has substantially widened the range of services that can be outsourced abroad, the economic characteristics and consequences of these activities are very similar to the long-standing historical process through which falling transportation costs have sharply expanded the range of goods subject to import competition. More generally, the substitution of imports for domestic production and offshoring are simply different forms of the same phenomenon. Increases in this kind of activity large enough to have a significant effect on US production and employment should generate corresponding increases in US imports of the relevant types of goods or services.

The immediate effect of an increase in offshoring is a reduction in US employment, either through a rise in worker layoffs or a slowdown in new job creation. Over the longer run, however, the lower prices for consumer and investment goods made possible by the offshoring raise real wages and living standards here at home while consumption and investment spending rise and employment recovers. This Policy Brief deals only with the short run negative effects on jobs.

Employment Effects of the Productivity Speedup

By the end of 2003, gross domestic product in the US nonfarm business sector had risen by more than 5 percent over the prior four quarters, and was almost 8 percent above what it had been three years before that at the peak of the boom. Yet the aggregate number of hours that employees worked had fallen by 4.5 percent—3 percent due to lower employment and 1.5 percent due to fewer average hours per week. An (admittedly mechanical) simulation can give some sense of the effect of the surge in productivity on the employment numbers. Productivity (output per hour) in the nonfarm business sector rose 2.6 percent a year between the fourth quarters of 1995 and 2000. In the next three years, it rose at a surprisingly strong 4.1 percent rate. If productivity growth over those three years had continued at its earlier pace, the aggregate hours of work needed to produce the fourth quarter 2003 GDP would have been more than 4.5 percent larger than it actually was. Employment in the nonfarm business sector would have been some 2 million persons higher, with the precise amount depending on just how much of the increase in total hours worked came from a recovery in the average length of the work week. The unemployment rate would probably have been somewhere around 5.0 percent.

If the alternative scenario had occurred, with its lower productivity growth and higher employment and worker income, the time-path of GDP itself would have been affected, although the extent and even the direction of the response is not obvious. But the alternative possibilities are irrelevant to the issue here: given the substantial growth of GDP that did occur, how much of the disappointing behavior of employment can be explained by acceleration of productivity as opposed to the growth of offshoring or other factors.

Without any increases in offshoring during the period, domestic production might have grown even faster than it did, with positive effects on employment. Nevertheless, had the nation experienced the millions of extra jobs, the rise in weekly hours, and the increase in wage and salary disbursements that would have occurred had productivity not accelerated, the media would now be paying far less attention to offshoring and low wage imports, and recent political rhetoric would not have so heavily featured the evils of NAFTA, Chinese competition, and offshoring.

The evidence about the dominating role of the recent productivity acceleration in explaining the jobless recovery does not address the size of employment effects on the increases in offshoring and import competition. Other evidence is needed to shed some light on this question.

Survey Evidence on Layoffs and Offshoring

The Bureau of Labor Statistics publishes a quarterly tabulation of "extended mass layoffs"—layoffs of fifty or more employees expected to last at least a month. Establishments that have made these layoffs are identified from federal and state unemployment insurance records, and are asked to assign the reason for them and to provide the total number laid off. Extended mass layoffs, for causes other than the ending of "seasonal" jobs, averaged 900,000 a year in 2002-2003. Among the relatively long list of reasons that respondents can assign for layoffs are "import competition" and "relocation overseas." Together, those two reasons accounted for only 4 percent of non-seasonal extended layoffs during this period.

These numbers, however, do not capture all of the layoffs and other effects on US employment from changes in overseas outsourcing and imports. They exclude smaller scale layoffs (less than fifty at a time). In some cases import competition can indirectly result in a loss of sales in ways that may not be apparent to or identified by the losing firm. Moreover, the estimates cannot pick up any effects on employment that show up, not in layoffs, but in a reduction of domestic hiring by offshoring firms that would otherwise have been adding to their workforce. Where outsourcing takes the form of contracting (directly or through intermediaries) with independent foreign suppliers, rather than transferring operations to majority-owned foreign affiliates, some respondents may not report this as a "relocation." But even after allowing for all of this, the data suggest, with respect to layoffs at least, that import competition and relocation play a much more modest role in explaining the jobless recovery than is depicted in much of the media.

Indirect Evidence from Import Data

The Overall Effect

When part of the production of goods or services destined for domestic markets is shifted abroad, the value of the outsourced production returns as imports. If the disappointing employment growth of the past several years came about because America's production needs were being met to an increasing degree by production from foreign rather than American workers, as Americans increased the share of consumer and capital goods they bought from abroad, or as domestic firms expanded the share of their operations located abroad, this should show up as a rise in the inflation-adjusted value of imports relative to GDP. During the 1990s the import share rose steadily, but apart from some short-term fluctuations the share leveled off thereafter. It is difficult from this data to see how changes in the combination of import substitution and offshoring could have played a major role in explaining America's job performance in recent years.

The estimates on imports of goods come from relatively comprehensive US customs data. Conceivably, the surveys of business firms used by the Department of Commerce to collect data on service imports may be missing some of the increase attributable to offshoring. I discuss later in this Policy Brief the issue of possible errors in the estimates of service imports. But the absolute size of any such errors in the import data cannot realistically be anywhere near large enough to alter the earlier conclusion that the speedup in productivity growth was by far the dominant factor behind the disappointing job growth.

Offshoring of Services

What can we say about the relative magnitude of the offshoring of services—software writers and computer technical support in India, clerical and record-keeping operations in the Caribbean, and call centers in a number of countries? Anecdotes abound, but was the growth of these operations sufficient to explain any significant part of the jobs problem? There is no fixed line of demarcation between offshoring activities and simple purchases of imported goods and services abroad. But the US data on imports of services suggests that the growth of those imports was not large enough to have made a major, economy-wide impact in swelling layoffs or inhibiting job growth.

Up-to-date quarterly estimates are available for imports of what are called "other services," that is, all services excluding travel, transportation, and royalty fees. Business, professional, and technical services (BPT for short), many of which have been subject to offshoring activities, account for a little more than half of "other private services," with the rest consisting of educational, financial, insurance, and telecommunication services that are not themselves likely to be heavily imported as a result of overseas relocations. Within the broad "other private services" category, the United States has long been running a substantial and growing export surplus. Between 1997 and 2003 imports did grow strongly, but in absolute terms, exports grew even faster, providing job opportunities that offset at least some of the job losses attributable to the rise in imports. Because the activities that are outsourced abroad are likely to use less skilled and lower-wage labor, it is possible that the job losses from offshoring exceeded the job gains associated with the growth in exports, but the magnitude of the net loss could not have been very large.

To make estimates about the level and growth of offshoring, it would be most useful to have import data classified at some greater level of detail, for example BPT services, and within that category specific information about such items as services related to computers, software, and data processing. Unfortunately, 2002 is the latest year for which complete data are available at that level of detail. BPT imports grew strongly in the five years preceding 2002, especially in the earlier part of the period, but here also the United States continued to run a large and gradually expanding export surplus. Between 1997 and 2002, imports of BPT services remained a virtually constant fraction of the larger category of "other private service" imports. If one assumes that this stability has continued, it is possible to get a reasonably good fix on the growth in BPT imports through the end of 2003. That data in turn can be used to make a rough calculation of the impact of the potential size of jobs lost to the offshoring of BPT services.

To give the offshoring hypothesis the benefit of the doubt, ignore any employment gains associated with growing exports of BPT services, and assume that all of the rise in imports in such services relative to GDP since the last quarter of 2000 was associated with growth in outsourcing activities involving a loss of domestic jobs among the firms involved. To make a crude estimate of the possible substitution of foreign workers for US workers, further assume that the number of displaced US workers equaled the number of foreign workers hired; that the relocated operations typically involved lower skilled jobs with about two-thirds to four-fifths of the value produced per worker than the average for the US "business services" industry; that the compensation per worker paid in the overseas locations ranged between one-fourth and one-sixth of US compensation; and that all other costs of the offshore services were close to what they would be in the United States. Given these alternative assumptions, the increased imports between the end of 2000 and the end of 2003 imply an aggregate job loss from outsourcing of BPT services alone totaling between 155,000 and 215,000.

These are necessarily very rough estimates, based on some judgmental assumptions. Some Indian estimates, which I discuss later, give the number of Indian employees associated with the relocation of computer and related operations to that country.

Depending on what one assumes about worker productivity in the Indian operations, those numbers suggest the possibility of somewhat larger numbers of job losses in the US information technology sector than implied by the estimates for BPT as a whole given above. But even substantially larger numbers would still be small in relation to the size of the US labor market and the magnitude of the annual job creation and destruction that characterizes the dynamic American economy.

A lot of the media attention has been focused on the relocation overseas of programming and other computer-related services. Imports of these services did rise sharply from 1997 through 2000, but the US data show no increase over the next two years. Given the sharp decline in the demand for information technology products after the high-tech bubble burst in 2001, the stability of imports of computer and related services from 2000 to 2002 probably conceals a continued rise in the importance of offshoring. At the same time, the continued high level of American sales abroad allowed the United States to continue running a substantial export surplus of these computer-related services.

In sum, what the US official trade data suggest is that the anecdotal evidence may indeed accurately reflect a substantial relative increase in the employment losses from the relocation of service-type activities abroad during recent years. But the data do not provide any evidence of an increase in offshoring of goods and services anywhere near large enough to have played a substantial role in shaping overall trends in US employment. Moreover, in the broad area of BPT services, where offshoring is most important, the United States has a large export market that continues to expand, providing a growing number of jobs for American workers.

The Official US Estimates

The data on imports and exports of BPT services are principally based on several surveys of business firms conducted by the Bureau of Economic Analysis. Substantial improvements have been made in the collection system over the last decade and a half. Nevertheless, an inspection of the data for India does raise some questions about the extent to which the data for particular categories of services are really capturing the rise in offshoring. The US data shows a substantial decline in "other service imports" from India between 2000 and 2002, which is hard to square with the abundance of anecdotes and media attention. US data covering unaffiliated trade with India in the more narrow category of BPT services (which is almost surely dominated by computer and related services) shows only $209 million in imports from India in 2002, about the same as in 2000. (Total service imports by US multinationals from their Indian affiliates were not large enough to add much to these figures).

The low $209 million level of non-affiliated BPT and computer related imports in the US data—and the absence of growth between 2000 and 2002—are impossible to reconcile with the anecdotal evidence. More importantly, data from Indian sources show a far higher level and a larger rate of increase in computer-related service exports to the United States than do the US import statistics.

According to Indian data, exports to the United States of computer software and other information technology related services—a subcategory within business services—amounted to $1.1 billion in 1997-98, $3.7 billion in fiscal year 2000/2001, and $6.0 billion in 2002/2003, many times higher than shown in the US import statistics. But these Indian data count as an export the revenue from arrangements whereby Indian firms, using Indian personnel, perform services at the US site of their clients. In the US data, the value of such services performed in this country are generally counted not as imports but as domestic production. Even after correcting for this difference, however, Indian computer and related service imports to the US rose from $1.6 to $3.4 billion between 2000/2001 and 2002/2003, a level and a rate of increase much higher than implied by the US import figures. And based on estimates derived from Indian data, the number of workers employed in producing computer and related services relocated from the United States to India could have increased by roughly 185,000 over the past four years.

It is not necessarily the case that it is the Indian data which are more nearly correct. There may be definitional reasons for some of the differences. And according to the data from Organization for Economic Cooperation and Development, the major industrial countries report imports of services from India that, in the aggregate, are a puzzlingly small fraction of the worldwide exports of services reported by India. But we do not know enough to form a good judgment. For a number of reasons, not least being the national attention paid to the offshoring phenomenon, we ought to have more information about this issue. Funds should be quickly provided to the BEA for a targeted research effort aimed at uncovering the reasons for the apparent discrepancy among different sources, and recommending any needed improvements in the US data collection system.

Should it should turn out that the official estimates are seriously understating the relevant service imports, the assessment of the employment effects of offshoring made earlier in this Policy Brief and elsewhere, based on evidence from US import data, would have to be significantly raised. But even a large increase in the estimate of the relevant service imports and their employment effects would still be quite small relative to the overall economy, the annual turnover in the American labor market, and the magnitude of the shortfall in job growth that has to be explained. Thus, for example, a large correction in the estimate of imports of BPT services, which are themselves only 0.4 percent of GDP, would imply only a very minor change in the reported acceleration of productivity growth over the last few years and its contribution to the slow recovery in employment until just recently.

The essential conclusion remains that offshoring, and more broadly import competition, while clearly having an important effect on some industries, workers, and communities, were not significant causes of the "jobless recovery."

Offshoring Has Helped the United States Reach Consumers in China and India

Ann All

Ann All worked as an associate editor at IT Business Edge.

Offshoring has become a well-accepted business practice in the United States, with many American companies taking advantage not only of lower-cost labor pools but also of skill sets in short supply in the United States. Yet it has remained a politically charged practice, and companies that offshore operations frequently face criticism from trade associations, commentators and, especially during election season, political candidates.

This year's presidential election, pitting Republican John McCain vs. Democrat Barack Obama, is no exception. Obama has yet to come up with a sound bite as memorable as the one used by two-time presidential candidate Ross Perot, who warned that jobs heading south to Mexico following ratification of the North American Free Trade Agreement in 1992 would create a "giant sucking sound."

Obama has followed the example of John Kerry, the Democrat who made offshoring-related criticism of President George W. Bush a regular part of his campaign appearances during the 20014 campaign. Kerry found receptive audiences, especially in states like Ohio and Pennsylvania, where local economies were hit hard by the loss of manufacturing jobs over the previous decade. His plan to address offshoring revolved around changing rules that allow American companies to defer paying taxes on income earned by foreign subsidiaries until they bring those profits back to the United States.

Bush's support for such rules encouraged the export of American jobs, said Kerry. Instead of Kerry-style denunciation

"Outrage Over Offshoring Goes Off-Target," by Ann All, Yale University, October 17, 2008. Reprinted by permission.

of unpatriotic companies offshoring their operation, Obama emphasizes positive incentives to those who don't.

As the US economy continues to sour in the wake of the credit crisis, Obama has used an anti-offshoring message that echoes Kerry's though on the campaign trail, his speeches are more nuanced. During his nomination speech at the Democratic National Convention, Obama said that "companies that ship jobs overseas will not get tax breaks."

His remarks were widely aired in India, a popular destination for companies that offshore information technology positions. Not all Indians appear concerned. Som Mittal, chairman of the country's National Association and Software Companies, said: "Democratic governments in the past were in support of free trade as the US has been all along. We don't think that practice will go when a new administration takes over early next year. The stakeholders are well aware of the advantages of outsourcing, especially in the service industry."

Obama in August 2007 introduced the Patriot Employer Act, which would offer tax breaks for US corporations that keep their headquarters on American shores, maintain a certain ratio of US-based employees to foreign employees and provide certain other employee benefits. Obama also said he would consider renegotiating NAFTA to include stricter environmental and labor standards. During the Democratic primary, he used opponent Hillary Clinton's past support for NAFTA to cast her as a candidate who cared more about big business than "ordinary" Americans.

During a speech to the International Association of Machinists and Aerospace Workers at its annual convention in September, Obama referred to a strike by Boeing machinists, during which the union has asked the company to agree to future limits on outsourcing. Obama said: "I support you because what you're fighting for is a fair shot at the American dream. It's the idea that your government shouldn't stand idly by while your job is shipped overseas."

Though Obama has supported trade deals with Peru and Oman, he opposes proposed agreements with Colombia and Panama and voted against the Central American Free Trade Agreement in 2005, which extended free trade to the Dominican Republic and other Central American countries. He may have had second thoughts on CAFTA, however, writing in his 2008 book "Change We Can Believe In" that CAFTA "was probably a net plus for the US economy."

Republican McCain, in contrast, has been a staunch supporter of free trade throughout his 22-year tenure in the Senate. In July, he visited Colombia to urge passage of the Colombia agreement. Before his trip, acknowledging that it might be difficult to sell Americans on the merits of another trade deal during the economic downturn, he said: "I have to convince them the consequences of protectionism and isolationism could be damaging to their future."

McCain voted for CAFTA and NAFTA and for expanded trade with Oman, Singapore, Chile, China, Vietnam and the Andean nations. In 1997, he voted to renew a "fast track" system that gave then-President Bill Clinton the ability to quickly negotiate free trade deals like NAFTA. In 2002, he voted to make trade agreements exempt from Congressional amendments. He also voted to kill a bill that would have imposed trade sanctions on China if the country didn't revalue its currency.

Like Bush before him, McCain emphasizes retraining American workers who lose their jobs due to offshoring. According to his campaign website, he'd overhaul the unemployment insurance program to do so.

The trade issue likely strikes a chord with at least some Americans, especially those in the battleground states of Ohio and Pennsylvania. In a 2005 Program on International Policy Attitudes poll, just 16 percent of respondents favored a liberal approach to trade, while 56 percent said they supported expanded trade, but only if more was done to assist US workers whose jobs are affected.

In a CBS News poll from August, 62 percent of Americans said the economic rise of countries like China and India has been "bad" for the US economy, while 14 percent said it has been "good." Addressing the question of whether free trade presents an opportunity or a threat to America's economy, respondents to a CNN poll were neutral last October. In June, their attitude shifted to slightly pessimistic.

Yet there is little hard evidence that offshoring results in a wholesale loss of American jobs. Canadian economists Runjuan Liu and Daniel Trefler published research concluding that US jobs lost due to offshoring to China and India are offset by the growing sales of US-produced services in those countries. Wrote the two, "…we can say with confidence that even if service trade with China and India grows at its current clip, the labor-market implications will be small."

University of Hawaii professor Raymond Panko reached a similar conclusion after studying data from the Bureau of Labor Statistics' Mass Layoff Statistics program, which tracks layoffs of 50 or more jobs. Of the nearly 1 million jobs lost since 2004, according to Panko, only 16,197 can be attributed to offshoring. Acknowledging that it's a small sample, as mass layoffs only account for some 5 percent of US job losses every year, Panko nonetheless suggests the data shows "no support for the idea that enormous numbers of IT jobs are being offshored." and writes, "This does not mean that offshoring is negligible—only that it does not appear to be large compared to total employment or total IT employment."

Though global trade is overshadowed for now by the broadening credit crisis and its impact on the world's financial markets, there seems to be little question that it will reassert itself as an important economic issue. Among the issues the newly-elected president will need to address: concern that the US could lose its edge in high-tech innovation; downward wage pressure, caused at least partly by the growing global labor market; and huge annual trade deficits.

Offshoring Is Necessary to Help Companies Compete in the Global Economy

T. J. Pestano

T. J. Pestano is a senior recruitment relationship manager at Manila Recruitment.

As businesses around the world seek growth and success, more and more companies are opting to hire offshore employees in the Philippines who will help them hit their goals while keeping costs to a minimum.

With the rapid advancement of communication technology, companies are now more equipped to set up offshore operations without sacrificing quality and productivity.

If you're a business owner looking for opportunities to advance your company's growth, relocating some of your operations overseas is one strategy that you can look into. Offshoring is proven to have numerous benefits that allow companies to continue growing and remain profitable. Here are some of them.

Business Growth

With the help of your offshore team, you are more capable of working on your deliverables with increased efficiency. This is an opportunity to scale your operations and expand your business services and offerings.

Having an offshore team also increases your capacity to take in more work—resulting in more profit for the company.

Reduced Costs

Lower operation cost is perhaps the most enticing advantage of offshore labor. Hiring offshore employees can significantly reduce costs in infrastructure, equipment, utilities, and employee salaries, among others.

"How Offshore Employees Benefit Your Business," by TJ Pestano, Manila Recruitment, September 22, 2017. Reprinted by permission.

According to an article published in the *Economist*, setting up operations overseas helps companies save over 30% even after training and infrastructure expenses. With the reduced costs, you can allocate more funds for investments and other more important expenses.

Control from Miles Away

When setting up offshore operations, you don't need to give up control or sacrifice the quality of your work output. Even when you're miles away, you can still provide direction to your offshore employees since you're still in charge of their training and development.

Retaining control of both your in-house and offshore operations ensures that your business endeavors are aligned, and all your employees are working towards the same goals. Additionally, it guarantees that the output produced by both teams is on par with your company's standards.

Greater Market Opportunity

Having teams in different countries enable you to reach more potential clients. You can raise more awareness about your business, and at the same time, establish your company as a global brand.

Dedicated Staff to Your Company

One of the definite perks of hiring an offshore team is having access to a vast pool of highly skilled and educated talents. Bringing in skills and ideas from individuals across the globe gives your company a globally competitive edge.

Moreover, offshore employees can offer fresh perspectives and unique ways to solve problems.

Availability in Different Locations

As you set up shop in different parts of the world, you create a workforce that is ready for 24/7 operations. This allows you to provide better support to your clients and customers whenever they need it.

Again, being visible in different locations raises awareness about your company and increase your chance to get the attention of potential clients.

Wider Access to Resources

Apart from getting an opportunity to connect with professionals with hard-to-find skills and competencies, offshoring also allows you to access resources that may not be available in your area.

From supplies to technology, resources that may be difficult to acquire in your locality will surely be available somewhere around the globe.

Opportunity to Focus on More Complex Tasks

Administrative tasks such as record keeping and payroll accounting can be delegated to your offshore staff. Other time-consuming business processes such as recruitment and management can also be assigned to your offshore team—allowing you and your in-house staff to focus on more complex tasks and projects.

Further, relieving your onsite team of mundane responsibilities can increase their engagement at work.

Offshoring is a win-win situation for everyone. For employees, it's an opportunity to improve their skills at a job that will provide them with a relatively more competitive salary. On the other hand, consumers are offered better products and services because of more efficient business operations. Finally, for the companies, offshoring is an opportunity to meet, if not exceed, business expectations without going over budget.

Through offshoring, businesses can work with skilled individuals from various parts of the world while maintaining the highest standard of work quality and productivity.

If you're going to ask recruitment consultants, they will surely say the same thing—offshoring is one of your business' gateways to success.

Offshore Practices Like Foreign Tax Havens Affect Domestic Tax Revenue

Tim Hyde

Tim Hyde is a doctoral student of economics at Carnegie Mellon University. He served as the American Economic Association web editor from 2015 to 2017.

The mega-leak of 11.5 million documents known as the Panama Papers revealing the existence and ownership of thousands of offshore companies with hidden assets has created headaches for politicians and billionaires whose names appear in the disclosures. It has also spurred a larger conversation about the growing problem of the tax haven economy.

Typical people aren't well-versed in anonymous shell companies, discretionary trusts, undeclared bank accounts, and the other tools that corporations and wealthy individuals use to legally (and illegally) skirt US tax laws, so advocates are trying to take advantage of the Panama Papers coverage to raise the profile of this issue. The last week has seen a new wave of pressure on politicians to close the legal loopholes in the system and make sure companies and high-net-worth individuals can't take advantage of offshore financial acrobatics to dramatically reduce their tax bills.

But it is hard to even get a handle on this problem without understanding the scope of the offshore economy. How much tax revenue is being lost to offshore tax havens? How much ingenuity and effort is being spent on schemes to shelter corporate profits? A 2014 article from the *Journal of Economic Perspectives* traces the history of the offshore economy and provides some estimates of its size.

In *Taxing across Borders: Tracking Personal Wealth and Corporate Profits*, author Gabriel Zucman argues that the problem of tax havens can actually be traced back to standards promulgated in the 1920s by the long-defunct League of Nations. At the time, many high-income nations had recently instituted corporate taxes and were struggling with questions about how and where to tax multinational corporations. Suppose a US corporation called USCorp starts operating in the UK and making money—which government should get to tax the resulting profits?

In response, The League commissioned a team of four economists to propose guidelines for nations to bring their tax policies into accordance. The economists reasoned that profits should be taxed at the source: if USCorp is producing and selling products in the UK with local raw materials and a staff stationed in the UK, then the UK, not the US, should have the right to tax those profits.

But what if USCorp produces goods in the UK and then ships them across the Atlantic to be sold in the States? Then are the profits American or British? The new guidelines said that the US and UK arms of USCorp should be treated as different companies and profits should be computed as if the UK arm had "sold" its goods to the US arm at a fair price.

To smooth out any problems or confusion with these principles, the new guidelines said, countries should sign bilateral treaties with each other to make clear the rules for corporations to avoid double taxation. In the subsequent years, countries signed thousands of inconsistent bilateral treaties to establish rules for how profits would be counted, apportioned between countries, and finally taxed.

These guidelines shaped the earliest corporate tax laws and are still generally reflected in those laws today. But in a world where modern communications technology allows individuals to incorporate a company in the Caribbean and a bank account in Switzerland in a matter of days, the conventions of corporate taxation that have prevailed for decades are increasingly easy to exploit.

Inconsistencies in tax treaties between different pairs of countries allow corporations to slip into legal netherworlds where their profits aren't generated in any particular country and can mostly escape taxation.

Google is a high-profile example: it is able to claim billions of profits in Bermuda each year (corporate tax rate: 0%) even though it has no office building there and not even any employees on the island. This seems to violate the spirit of the source-based taxation guidelines originating in the 1920s, because only a very small fraction of Google's profits from online advertising sales are actually coming from the small island nation of Bermuda.

But this is legitimate because the rights to Google's search and advertising technologies are technically owned by a subsidiary called Google Holdings housed in Bermuda, thanks in part to a trick called the Double Irish Dutch Sandwich. Other Google subsidiaries pay billions in royalties to the Bermudian company Google Holdings for the rights to use its technology, which was originally invented by Google employees in California and sold to Google Holdings in 2001. Those billions of profits are reclassified as Bermudian rather than American or Irish and thus not taxed.

Countries can rework their laws and treaties to try to close loopholes once they are discovered, but legal teams will keep working to exploit any inconsistencies in treaties that allow profits to be booked in lower-tax countries without actually having to move any substantial operations to these often-remote tax havens. The result is that American-controlled corporations in places like the Cayman Islands or the British Virgin Islands often earn profits that are greater than the gross domestic products of these island nations.

Offshore machinations reduce government revenues that could offset other taxes and fund public services, but they also induce a wasteful response by corporations that has its own non-negligible cost. There are thousands, perhaps even millions, of people around the world who spend their working lives devising tax-reduction schemes, fielding phone calls or handling paperwork to establish offshore accounts, or preparing the complicated tax returns required to sustain these schemes. Even for those who believe corporate taxes are too high, allowing offshore tax havens to effectively reduce corporate tax bills is far less efficient than actually reducing the statutory rate.

Zucman's analysis shows that this problem has grown more acute in recent years. By analyzing data from the National Income and Product Accounts that estimate overall corporate profits accruing to US residents, and comparing these figures to corporate tax filings and US tax receipts, Zucman can compare the statutory tax rate with what actually gets paid. The nominal corporate tax rate has been 35% since 1993, but the proportion of US corporate profits actually collected by the IRS (the effective tax rate) has never reached even 30% in the years since that change and in 2013 stood around 16%.

This discrepancy can't be blamed entirely on offshore tax havens—some is attributable to other tax breaks like deductions for manufacturing income or writeoffs for capital losses during the Great Recession—but Zucman estimates that offshore tax schemes are responsible for about two-thirds of the decline in the effective tax rate since 1998, representing a loss of over $100 billion for the US treasury in 2013.

What can be done to shut down offshore tax havens? Zucman points out there is no shortage of proposals for reforming the corporate tax system by abandoning the old principles set out by the League of Nations nearly a century ago. Some have advocated a push to make tax treaties between countries more consistent and leave less room for corporations to slip through the cracks. Others have proposed a different taxation scheme that divvies up a corporation's tax bill across countries based on its local sales or the location of its employees—Google wouldn't be able to claim profits in Bermuda without actually having a substantial presence there.

Zucman closes with a reminder of the stakes for reforming the international corporate tax system and the shadowy tax havens that allow corporations to avoid taxes. After all, many of the same tricks that allow major corporations to shelter profits in offshore shell companies allow criminal enterprises to launder money or funnel support to terrorist organizations. The Panama Papers leak is a rare opportunity for policymakers to shine a light on this growing problem and reform a creaky global corporate tax system that is showing its age.

One-Fifth of American Jobs Are at Risk of Being Offshored

Ron Hira

Ron Hira, who is the coauthor of Outsourcing America, *works as an assistant professor of public policy at Rochester Institute of Technology.*

Offshoring is the movement of jobs and tasks from one country to another, usually from high-cost countries, such as the United States, to low-cost countries where wages are significantly lower. Offshoring is often confused with outsourcing, which is instead the movement of jobs and tasks from within a company to a supplier firm. The offshoring of manufacturing jobs has been occurring for decades, but the offshoring of service-sector jobs is an incipient phenomenon, emerging in substantial numbers since 2002 and growing rapidly.

Which Jobs and How Much

While there is widespread interest in measuring offshoring, available government data have significant limitations, making it nearly impossible to get an accurate picture of its scale and scope.[1] The table below shows the results of an exploratory study by Princeton University economist Alan Blinder that attempts to fill this void. He estimates the 10 most vulnerable occupations, where US workers in these jobs now face competition from overseas workers. Blinder estimates that about 30 million jobs, accounting for a little more than one-fifth of the US workforce, are vulnerable to offshoring.

Most studies identify whether the work can be done remotely and whether it can be easily reduced to a set of written rules and procedures as determining the likelihood that a job or activity may

"Offshoring US Labor Increasing," by Ron Hira, Population Reference Bureau, October 2008. Reprinted by permission.

Occupations Most Vulnerable to Offshoring

RANK	OCCUPATION	ANNUAL MEAN WAGE	NUMBER EMPLOYED
1	Computer programmers	$72,010	394,710
2	Data entry keyers	$26,350	286,540
3	Electrical and electronics drafters	$51,710	32,350
4	Mechanical drafters	$46,690	74,260
5	Computer and information	$100,640	28,720
6	Actuaries	$95,420	18,030
7	Mathematicians	$90,930	3,160
8	Statisticians	$72,150	20,270
9	Mathematical science occupations (all other)	$61,100	6,930
10	Film and video editors	$61,180	17,410

SOURCES: Alan S. Blinder, "How Many US Jobs Might Be Offshorable?" *CEPS Working Paper 142* (March 2007); and Bureau of Labor Statistics, *National Occupational Employment and Wage Estimates*, May 2007 (www.bls.gov/oes/current/oes_nat.htm, accessed May 28, 2008).

be transferred to another country. An occupation that requires being physically present with a customer is less vulnerable because it cannot be done remotely. Work which requires judgment combined with a deep understanding of the customer's cultural context is difficult to do remotely because it cannot be easily written into a set of rules and protocols.

One important finding of many of the forecasts is that a large share of vulnerable jobs pay high wages and require advanced education (as shown in the table), making it more difficult to predict the overall impact of offshoring on the US economy and to devise appropriate policy responses.

Why Offshore

Firms use offshore jobs to reduce costs. A typical accountant in India earns about $5,000 per year, whereas a US accountant earns about \$63,000.[2] These large wage differentials make it very attractive for companies to lower costs by substituting US workers with lower-cost overseas workers. As the CEO of a major technology company put it, "If you can find high quality talent at a third of the price, it's not too hard to see why you'd do this [send jobs offshore]."[3] By lowering costs through offshoring, firms can gain a business advantage over their competitors.

Some factors that influence offshoring are driven by markets while others are based on government intervention. Companies selling to an overseas market sometimes find it easier to use local workers to customize a product because they better understand the tastes of the customers. Also, the markets in many emerging countries with a burgeoning new consumer class, such as India and China, are growing at three to four times the rate of markets in developed countries in North America and Europe. In other cases, governments are actively pursuing offshore outsourcing of US and European jobs by offering an array of incentives, such as tax holidays (where the firm pays no income or property taxes), new facilities at reduced rates, and training subsidies. And some countries require the transfer of technology and high-wage jobs as a condition for selling in their markets.

US government tax and immigration policies are actually speeding up offshoring. US-based multinational corporations that outsource work offshore receive tax breaks.[4] And offshore outsourcing firms have exploited loopholes in US immigration policy, particularly in the H-1B and L-1 guest worker visas, to facilitate the transfer of work overseas.[5]

Major changes in technology and social norms have enabled offshoring. Technological breakthroughs in telecommunications, the Internet, and collaborative software tools have dramatically lowered the costs of doing business remotely and across borders.

Additionally, shifts in employment relations and norms have made it much easier for firms to substitute foreign workers for US workers.

Which Industries and Where

Information technology (IT) services was the first industrial sector to move a significant number of jobs offshore. Labor costs, which are often 70 percent of the net cost for IT firms, make the sector ripe for offshoring. Other information-intensive sectors, such as insurance and financial services, are aggressively offshoring. While not well publicized, occupations in a wide variety of other sectors (for example, journalism, law, medicine, and animation) are also moving offshore.

India has been the major beneficiary of white-collar offshoring from the United States, but almost every other developing country is trying to replicate India's success. India has many advantages, including its large English-speaking educated workforce, its large diaspora living in the United States and the UK, and its specialization in IT. Western Europe is about three to five years behind the United States in offshoring due to language barriers and greater protection for their domestic workers. But this phenomenon is growing in importance both economically and politically there as well.

References

1. Timothy J. Sturgeon, "Why We Can't Measure the Economic Effects of Services Offshoring: The Data Gaps and How to Fill Them," *Services Offshoring Working Group Final Report*, (Cambridge, MA: Industrial Performance Center, Massachusetts Institute of Technology, Sept. 10, 2006).

2. India wage based on author's estimates. US wage source: Bureau of Labor Statistics, *National Occupational Employment and Wage Estimates*, May 2007.

3. Brian Jackson, "EDS Says Offshoring Great for Profitability, Promises to Continue," *ITBusiness.ca* (Canada), April 23, 2008.

4. Kimberly A. Clausing, "The Role of US Tax Policy in Offshoring," in *Brookings Trade Forum: Offshoring White-Collar Work,* ed. Lael Brainard and Susan M. Collins (Washington, DC: Brookings Institution Press, 2006).

5. Ron Hira, "Outsourcing America's Technology and Knowledge Jobs: High-Skill Guest Worker Visas Are Currently Hurting Rather Than Helping Keep Jobs at Home," *EPI Briefing Paper* 187 (March 28, 2007).

Offshoring Continues to Put a Lot of Pressure on American Workers

Paul Craig Roberts

Paul Craig Roberts is the author of the book How The Economy Was Lost. *He was also assistant secretary of the treasury under the Reagan administration.*

Is offshore outsourcing good or harmful for America? To convince Americans of outsourcing's benefits, corporate outsourcers sponsor misleading one-sided "studies."

Only a small handful of people have looked objectively at the issue. These few and the large number of Americans whose careers have been destroyed by outsourcing have a different view of outsourcing's impact. But so far there has been no debate, just a shouting down of skeptics as "protectionists."

Now comes an important new book, Outsourcing America, published by the American Management Association. The authors, two brothers, Ron and Anil Hira, are experts on the subject. One is a professor at the Rochester Institute of Technology, and the other is professor at Simon Fraser University.

The authors note that despite the enormity of the stakes for all Americans, a state of denial exists among policymakers and outsourcing's corporate champions about the adverse effects on the US. The Hira brothers succeed in their task of interjecting harsh reality where delusion has ruled.

In what might be an underestimate, a University of California study concludes that 14 million white-collar jobs are vulnerable to being outsourced offshore. These are not only call-center operators, customer service and back-office jobs, but also information technology, accounting, architecture, advanced engineering design, news reporting, stock analysis, and medical and legal

"The Offshore Outsourcing of American Jobs: A Greater Threat Than Terrorism," by Dr. Paul Craig Roberts, GlobalResearch, March 13, 2016. Reprinted by permission.

services. The authors note that these are the jobs of the American Dream, the jobs of upward mobility that generate the bulk of the tax revenues that fund our education, health, infrastructure, and social security systems.

The loss of these jobs "is fool's gold for companies." Corporate America's short-term mentality, stemming from bonuses tied to quarterly results, is causing US companies to lose not only their best employees-their human capital-but also the consumers who buy their products. Employees displaced by foreigners and left unemployed or in lower paid work have a reduced presence in the consumer market. They provide fewer retirement savings for new investment.

Nothink economists assume that new, better jobs are on the way for displaced Americans, but no economists can identify these jobs. The authors point out that "the track record for the re-employment of displaced US workers is abysmal: "The Department of Labor reports that more than one in three workers who are displaced remains unemployed, and many of those who are lucky enough to find jobs take major pay cuts. Many former manufacturing workers who were displaced a decade ago because of manufacturing that went offshore took training courses and found jobs in the information technology sector. They are now facing the unenviable situation of having their second career disappear overseas."

American economists are so inattentive to outsourcing's perils that they fail to realize that the same incentive that leads to the outsourcing of one tradable good or service holds for all tradable goods and services. In the 21st century the US economy has only been able to create jobs in nontradable domestic services-the hallmark of a third world labor force.

Prior to the advent of offshore outsourcing, US employees were shielded against low wage foreign labor. Americans worked with more capital and better technology, and their higher productivity protected their higher wages.

Outsourcing forces Americans to "compete head-to-head with foreign workers" by "undermining US workers' primary competitive advantage over foreign workers: their physical presence in the US" and "by providing those overseas workers with the same technologies."

The result is a lose-lose situation for American employees, American businesses, and the American government. Outsourcing has brought about record unemployment in engineering fields and a major drop in university enrollments in technical and scientific disciplines. Even many of the remaining jobs are being filled by lower paid foreigners brought in on H-1b and L-1 visas. American employees are discharged after being forced to train their foreign replacements.

US corporations justify their offshore operations as essential to gain a foothold in emerging Asian markets. The Hira brothers believe this is self-delusion. "There is no evidence that they will be able to outcompete local Chinese and Indian companies, who are very rapidly assimilating the technology and know-how from the local US plants. In fact, studies show that Indian IT companies have been consistently outcompeting their US counterparts, even in US markets. Thus, it is time for CEOs to start thinking about whether they are fine with their own jobs being outsourced as well."

The authors note that the national security implications of outsourcing "have been largely ignored."

Outsourcing is rapidly eroding America's superpower status. Beginning in 2002 the US began running trade deficits in advanced technology products with Asia, Mexico and Ireland. As these countries are not leaders in advanced technology, the deficits obviously stem from US offshore manufacturing. In effect, the US is giving away its technology, which is rapidly being captured, while US firms reduce themselves to a brand name with a sales force.

In an appendix, the authors provide a devastating expose of the three "studies" that have been used to silence doubts about offshore outsourcing-the Global Insight study (March 2004) for the Information Technology Association of America, the Catherine Mann study (December 2003) for the Institute for International

Economics, and the McKinsey Global Institute study (August 2003).

The ITAA is a lobbying group for outsourcing. The ITAA spun the results of the study by releasing only the executive summary to reporters who agreed not to seek outside opinion prior to writing their stories.

Mann's study is "an unreasonably optimistic forecast based on faulty logic and a poor understanding of technology and strategy."

The McKinsey report "should be viewed as a self-interested lobbying document that presents an unrealistically optimistic estimate of the impact of offshore outsourcing and an undeveloped and politically unviable solution to the problems they identify."

Outsourcing America is a powerful work. Only fools will continue clinging to the premise that outsourcing is good for America.

CHAPTER 4

Is Domestic Manufacturing Less Harmful to the Environment?

Overview: Climate Change Caused by Industrialization Affects the World's Biodiversity and Human Health

European Environment Agency

The European Environment Agency is a segment of the European Union. It helps the EU keep track of its environmental efforts.

There is a two-way relationship between Europe and the rest of the world. Europe is contributing to environmental pressures and accelerating feedbacks in other parts of the world through its dependence on fossil fuels, mining products and other imports. Conversely, in a highly interdependent world, changes in other parts of the world are increasingly felt closer to home, both directly through the impacts of global environmental changes, or indirectly through intensified socio-economic pressures.

Climate change is an obvious example. Most of the growth in global greenhouse gas emissions is projected to occur outside Europe, as a result of increasing wealth in populous emerging economies. In spite of successful efforts to reduce emissions and a decreasing share in the global total, European societies continue to be major emitters of greenhouse gases.

Many of the countries that are most vulnerable to climate change are outside the European continent, others are our direct neighbours. Often these countries are highly dependent on climate-sensitive sectors such as farming and fishing. Their adaptive capacity varies, but is often rather low, in particular due to persistent poverty. The links between climate change, poverty and political and security risks and their relevance for Europe have been extensively analysed.

Biodiversity has continued to decline globally despite a few encouraging achievements and increased policy action. The global rate of species extinction is escalating and is now estimated to be up to 1000 times the natural rate. Evidence is growing that critical ecosystem services are under great pressure globally. According to one estimate, approximately one quarter of the potential net primary production has been converted by humans, either through direct cropping (53%), land-use-induced productivity changes (40%) or human-induced fires (7%). While such figures should be treated with caution, they do give an indication of the substantial impact of humans on natur al ecosystems.

Loss of biodiversity in other regions of the world affects European interests in several ways. It is the world's poor that bear the brunt of biodiversity loss, as they are usually most directly reliant on functioning ecosystem services. Increases in poverty and inequality are likely to further fuel conflict and instability in regions that are already characterised by often fragile governance structures. Moreover, reduced genetic variety in crops and cultivars implies future losses of economic and social benefits for Europe in such critical areas as food production and modern healthcare.

Global extraction of natural resources from ecosystems and mines grew more or less steadily over the past 25 years, from 40 billion tonnes in 1980 to 58 billion tonnes in 2005. Resource extraction is unevenly distributed across the world, with Asia accounting for the largest share in 2005 (48% of total tonnage, compared with Europe's 13%). Over this period, a relative decoupling of global resource extraction and economic growth took place: resource extraction increased by roughly 50% and world economic output (GDP) by about 110%.

Nonetheless, resource use and extraction is still increasing in absolute terms, outweighing gains in resource efficiency. Such a composite indicator does not, however, reveal information on specific resource developments. Global food, energy and water systems appear to be more vulnerable and fragile than thought a few years ago, the factors responsible being increased demand, decreased supply, and supply instabilities. Over-exploitation, degradation and loss of soils are relevant concerns in this regard.

With global competition and increased geographic and corporate concentration of supplies for some resources, Europe faces increasing supply risks.

In spite of general progress in the area of environment and health in Europe, the global human toll of environmental health impacts remains deeply worrying. Unsafe water, poor sanitation and hygiene conditions, urban outdoor air pollution, indoor smoke from solid fuels and lead exposure and global climate change account for nearly a tenth of deaths and disease burden globally, and around one quarter of deaths and disease burden in children under 5 years of age. It is again poor populations in low latitudes that are affected most heavily.

Many low- and middle-income countries now face a growing burden from new risks to health, while still fighting an unfinished battle with the traditional risks to health. The World Health Organization (WHO) forecasts that between 2006 and 2015, deaths from non-communicable diseases could increase worldwide by 17%. The greatest increase is projected for the African region (24%) followed by the eastern Mediterranean region (23%). Europe is likely to be faced with the increased problem of emerging or re-emerging infectious diseases that are critically influenced by changes in temperature or precipitation, habitat loss and ecological destruction. In an increasingly urbanised world, which is tightly linked by long-distance transport, the incidence and distribution of infectious diseases affecting humans is likely to increase.

[…]

Environmental Challenges Are Closely Connected with Global Drivers of Change

A range of unfolding trends are shaping the future European and global context, and many of these are outside the realm of Europe's direct influence. Related global megatrends cut across social, technological, economic, political and even environment dimensions. Key developments include changing demographic patterns or accelerating rates of urbanisation, ever faster technological changes, deepening market integration, evolving economic power shifts or the changing climate.

A selection of global megatrends

- Increasing global divergence in population trends: populations ageing, growing and migrating
- Living in an urban world: spreading cities & spiralling consumption
- Changing patterns of global disease burdens and the risk of new pandemics
- Accelerating technologies: racing into the unknown
- Continued economic growth
- Global power shifts: from a uni-polar to a multi-polar world
- Intensified global competition for resources
- Decreasing stocks of natural resources
- Increasing severity of the consequences of climate change
- Increasingly unsustainable environmental pollution load
- Global regulation and governance: increasing fragmentation, but converging outcomes

In 1960, the world's population was 3 billion. Today, it is about 6.8billion. The United Nations Population Division expects this growth to continue and that the global population will exceed 9billion by 2050, according to the "medium growth variant" of their population estimate. However, uncertainties are apparent, and forecasts depend on several assumptions, including for fertility rates. As such, by 2050, the world population could thus exceed 11 billion or be limited to 8 billion. The implications of this uncertainty for global resource demands are huge.

In contrast to the global trend, European populations are expected to decline and age significantly. In its neighbourhood, population decline is particularly dramatic in Russia and large parts of Europe. At the same time, northern African countries along the southern Mediterranean are witnessing strong population growth. In general, the wider region of Northern Africa and the Middle East has experienced the highest rate of population growth of any region in the world over the past century.

The regional distribution of population growth, the age structure, and migration between regions are also important. Ninety percent of the population growth since 1960 has been in countries classified as "less developed" by the United Nations. Meanwhile, the world is urbanising at an unprecedented rate. By 2050, about 70% of the global population is likely to live in cities, compared with less than 30% in 1950. Population growth is now largely an urban phenomenon concentrated in the developing world, particular Asia, which is estimated to be home to more than 50% of the global urban population by 2050.

Global integration of markets, shifts in global competitiveness and changing global spending patterns comprise another complex set of drivers. As a result of liberalisation and due to the lowering of transport and communication costs, international trade over the past half-century has grown rapidly: global exports grew in value from USD296 billion in 1950 to more than USD8 trillion (measured in relation to "purchasing power parity") in 2005, and their share of global GDP rose from around 5% to close to 20%. Similarly, remittances sent home from emigrant workers often represent a large source of income for developing countries. For some countries remittances exceeded a quarter of the respective GDP in 2008 (for example, 50% in Tajikistan, 31% in Moldova, 28% in the Krygyz Republic, and 25% in Lebanon).

Aided by globalisation, many countries have been able to lift larger proportions of their populations out of poverty. Global economic growth and trade integration have fuelled long-term shifts in international competitiveness, characterised by a high growth of productivity in emerging economies. The number of middle-income consumers world-wide is growing rapidly, particularly in Asia. The World Bank has estimated that, by 2030, there could be 1.2billion middle-income consumers (C) in the emerging and developing economies of today. Already in 2010, the economies of the BRIC countries—Brazil, Russia, India and China—are expected to contribute almost half of global consumption growth.

Large differences in individual wealth accumulation are expected to persist between developed economies and key emerging economies. Yet the world's economic balance of power is changing. Large shifts in purchasing power towards middle-income economies and middle-income consumers are underway, creating significant consumer markets in emerging markets that are likely to fuel future global resource demands, again particularly in Asia. According to one estimate, the BRIC countries together could match the G7 share of global GDP by the 2040s.

A number of critical uncertainties are, however, embedded in those projections. Examples include uncertainties about the degree to which Asia might integrate economically, the impact of population ageing and the capacity to strengthen private investment and education. In the context of greater interconnectedness of markets and a higher susceptibility to risks of market failures, global regulatory regimes are likely to expand in the future, yet their contours and thus their role are unpredictable.

Furthermore, the speed and scope of scientific and technological progress influences key socio-economic trends and drivers. Eco-innovation and eco-friendly technologies are of key relevance in this regard; European companies are already relatively well-positioned in global markets. Supporting policies are relevant both in terms of facilitating market entry of new eco-innovations and technologies as well as increasing global demand.

In the longer-term perspective, developments and technology convergence in nanoscience and nanotechnologies, biotechnologies and life-sciences, information and communication technologies, cognitive sciences and neuro-technologies are expected to have profound effects on economies, societies and the environment. They are likely to open up completely new options for mitigating and remedying environmental problems including, for example, new pollution sensors, new types of batteries and other technologies for energy storage, and lighter and more durable materials for cars, buildings or aircrafts.

However, these technologies also give rise to concerns about detrimental effects on the environment, given the scale and level of complexity of their interactions. The existence of unknown, even unknowable, impacts poses a great challenge to risk governance. Rebound effects might also jeopardize environmental and resource-efficiency achievements.

As a result of demographic and economic power shifts, the contours of the global governance landscape are changing. A diffusion of political power towards multiple poles of influence is on-going, and changing the geo-political landscape. Private actors such as multi-national enterprises are playing an increasing role in world politics, and are becoming more directly involved in the formulation and implementation of policies. Fostered by advances in communications and information technology, civil society is also increasingly taking part in global negotiation processes of all kind. The interdependence and complexity of decision-making is growing as a result, giving rise to new modes of governance and posing new questions about responsibility, legitimacy and accountability.

Environmental Challenges May Increase Risks to Food, Energy and Water Security on a Global Scale

Global environmental challenges, such as impacts of climate change, loss of biodiversity, over-use of natural resources and environmental and health issues, are critically linked to issues of poverty and the sustainability of ecosystems, and consequently, issues of resource security and political stability. This adds pressure and uncertainty to the overall competition for natural resources, which might intensify as a consequence of increased demands, decreased supplies and decreased stability of supplies. Ultimately, this further increases pressure on ecosystems globally, and especially their capacity to ensure continued food, energy and water security.

According to the Food and Agriculture Organization of the United Nations (FAO), demand for food, feed and fibres could grow by 70% by 2050. The fragility of global food, water and energy systems has become apparent over recent years. For example, arable land per person declined globally from 0.43 ha in 1962 to 0.26 ha in 1998. The FAO expects this value to fall further by 1.5% per year between now and 2030, if no major policy changes are initiated.

Similarly, the International Energy Agency (IEA) expects global demand for energy to rise by 40% over the next 20 years if no major policy changes are implemented. The IEA has repeatedly warned about an impeding global energy crisis due to rising long-term demand. Massive and continuous investments are needed in energy efficiency, renewable energies and new infrastructures to achieve the transition to a low-carbon, resource efficient energy system that is compliant with long-term environmental objectives.

But it could be water shortages that will hit hardest over the coming decades. One estimate suggests that in just 20 years, global demand for water could be 40% higher than today, and more than 50% higher in the most rapidly developing countries. Furthermore, according to a recent estimate prepared by the Secretariat of the Convention of Biological Diversity, the flow in more than 60 per cent of the large river systems in the world has been heavily altered. Limits of ecological sustainability of water availability for abstraction have thus been reached, and up to 50% of the world could be living in areas with high water stress by 2030, while more than 60% could still lack improved access to sanitation.

Water infrastructure systems are often old and there is a lack of information about actual performance and losses. One estimate foresees an average annual investment need of USD772 billion for maintaining water and wastewater services around the world by 2015. Here, potential for ripple effects for food and energy supply exist, for example, cutting agricultural output which could result in decreasing overall social resilience.

Already today, in many parts of the world, non-renewable resource use is close to its limit and potentially renewable resources are being used beyond their reproductive capacity. This kind of dynamics can also be recognised in Europe's neighbouring regions with their comparatively rich natural capital. Water resource over-exploitation, combined with insufficient access to safe drinking water and sanitation, for example, are critical challenges both in Eastern Europe and the Mediterranean.

At the global level, poverty and social exclusion are further exacerbated by ecosystem degradation and changes in the climate. Globally, efforts to alleviate extreme poverty were reasonably effective until the 1990s. However, the recurring food and economic crises throughout 2006 to 2009 have magnified the trend of increasing under-nourishment rates around the world. The number of undernourished rose, for the first time, to more than 1 billion in 2009 and the proportion of undernourished in developing countries, which was declining quite rapidly, has risen in the past few years.

Resource over-exploitation and changes in the climate aggravate threats to natural capital. They also affect quality of life, potentially undermining social and political stability. Furthermore, the livelihoods of billions of people are inevitably linked with the sustainability of local ecosystem services. Combined with demographic pressures, decreasing socio-ecological resilience can add a new dimension to the environment and security debate, as conflict around scarcer resources is likely to intensify and add to migration pressures.

Global Developments May Increase Europe's Vulnerabilities to Systemic Risks

Since many of the global drivers of change operate beyond Europe's direct influence, Europe's vulnerability to external change could increase markedly, particularly accentuated by developments in its direct neighbourhood. Being a resource-scarce continent and neighbour to some of the world's regions most prone to global environmental change, active engagement and cooperation with these regions can help address the range of problems that Europe is facing.

Many key drivers operate on a global scale and are likely to unfold over decades rather than years. In a recent assessment, the World Economic Forum warned about a higher level of systemic risk due to the increase in interconnections among various risks. Furthermore, the assessment emphasised that unexpected, sudden changes in external conditions are inevitable in a highly inter-linked world. While sudden changes can have huge impacts, the biggest risks may be from slow failures which unfold their full damage potential over decades and may be seriously underestimated in their potential economic impact and societal cost. The continued over-exploitation of natural capital is an example for a slow failure.

Such systemic risks—whether they manifest themselves as sudden changes or slow failures—include the potential damage to, or even full failure of, an entire system, for example a market or an ecosystem, as opposed to effects on individual elements only. The interconnectedness between drivers and risks highlighted here are relevant in this regard: while these links can lead to higher robustness when risk sharing is distributed across a greater number of elements in the system, they can also lead to greater fragility. Failure in one critical link can have cascading effects, often as a consequence of decreased system diversity and governance gaps.

A key related risk is that of accelerating global environmental feedback mechanisms and their direct and indirect impacts on Europe. Since the Millennium Ecosystem Assessment (12) and the IPCCFourth Assessment Report, scientific assessments have warned that environmental feedback mechanisms are increasing the likelihood of large scale non-linear changes in key Earth system components. With increasing global temperatures, for example, there is an increasing risk of passing tipping points that may trigger large-scale, non-linear changes.

Systemic risks have the potential, if they are not properly addressed, to inflict devastating damage on the vital systems, natural capital and infrastructures on which our well-being depends both at a local and at a global scale. Thus, joint efforts are required to tackle some of the causes of systemic risks, develop adaptive management practices and strengthen resilience in view of increasingly pressing environmental challenges.

Environmental Regulations in the United States Help Control Pollution

Mary Graham

Mary Graham codirects the Transparency Policy Project at Harvard's Kennedy School. She has been published by the Brookings Institution, Atlantic Monthly, *and* Financial Times.

When Congress laid the foundation for today's environmental regulation in the early 1970s, the idea that states inevitably cut corners in pollution control and conservation to attract business was a powerful argument for national action. When industrial debris in Cleveland's Cuyahoga River caught fire and oil from an offshore blowout blighted Santa Barbara's beaches in 1969, the incidents became national symbols of a "race to the bottom" in state and local politics.

Recently, this view has gained new support. Not long ago, the press carried graphic accounts of hog wastes washing down Virginia's Pagan River toward the Chesapeake Bay from a plant owned by Smithfield Foods, Inc., the East Coast's largest producer of pork products. Lax state enforcement of national water pollution laws "could create 'pollution havens'" and "lead to a shift of manufacturing and jobs that would penalize the conscientious states," the New York Times editorialized.

But the race to the bottom idea is too simplistic to describe the forces that shape state environmental policies in the 1990s. The idea is outdated for three reasons. First, evidence is by now overwhelming that businesses rarely decide where to locate or expand based on the strength or weakness of state environmental programs. Second, state politics have been transformed in ways that make it more likely that pollution and conservation issues will

"Environmental Protection & the States: 'Race to the Bottom' or 'Race to the Bottom Line'?" by Mary Graham, The Brookings Institution, December 1, 1998. Reprinted by permission.

get a fair hearing, independent of federal action. Finally, and most important, public attitudes have changed. Today, states compete to gain prosperity in a fast-changing economy. After nearly 30 years of government action and scientific progress, government officials, business executives, and voters find that some environmental measures aid in that contest. There is growing evidence that some states lead in economic growth and environmental protection, while other states lag behind in both.

To call attention to these changes is not to deny that state and local governments face tough trade-offs, that businesses often lobby to weaken environmental rules, or that some polluters still try to beat the system. Hiring inspectors to enforce the law or buying land to protect a watershed is expensive and must vie for limited state funds with improving schools, building roads, and paying for Medicaid and welfare. Environmental issues continue to be contentious because they often do pit jobs against cleaner air or more conservation, and sometimes both choices offer economic benefits. When stakes are high, business, labor, homeowners, and other groups will fight for their interests. And, of course, there will always be cheaters.

Thirty years ago, the assumption that there was a race to the bottom among the states was important because Congress was debating the need for a national framework of environmental protection. That question is now settled. Mainstream Democrats and Republicans agree that air pollution, water pollution, and other environmental problems that cross state lines should continue to be controlled by federal rules. Because most of our daily attention is drawn to hard-fought battles at the perimeter of government authority, it is easy to forget that we have witnessed an exceptional event in the past three decades: the successful introduction of a new theme in national policy.

Today, the question of whether states shortchange environmental protection to attract business is important for different reasons. First, we have reached a turning point in national environmental policy in which some readjustment of federal and state roles is inevitable. Thanks in part to the considerable success of national laws aimed at controlling major sources of pollution and encouraging conservation on large tracts of federal land, public attention is now turning to problems that are harder to solve from Washington. The next generation of environmental policies will tackle widely scattered sources of pollution and conservation opportunities that affect farms and housing developments as well as forests and meadows.

Second, both Democrats and Republicans are calling for new approaches to the first generation of environmental problems in order to give more flexibility to states. Frustration with the high costs and rigidity of "command and control" regulations has prompted moves to supplement those rules with market incentives, negotiated agreements, industry standards, and other techniques that decentralize decisions.

Third, the reach of federal regulation may be overly broad. The National Academy of Public Administration has suggested, for example, that controlling chemical contaminants in drinking water and deciding when, where, and how to clean up hazardous waste might better be done by state and local governments.

Continuing confusion about the capabilities of state governments is costly. Much-needed revisions of three of the legal cornerstones of national environmental policy – the Superfund, Clean Water, and Endangered Species Acts – are stalled in Congress in part because of troublesome questions about how federal and state governments should share authority.

Businesses Have Changes

In the 1970s, sudden new pollution control requirements with short deadlines called for large, unplanned investments that were extremely costly to some industries. Today, environmental costs rarely determine business location because they have become a relatively small and usually predictable element of corporate expenses. Even for chemical and petroleum industries, annual pollution abatement expenses run less than 2 percent of sales.

Capital costs for pollution control vary widely from one industry to another, ranging from 2 percent of total capital costs for machinery and 3 percent for electronics to 13 percent for chemical industries and 25 percent for petroleum and coal. Even when substantial, though, those costs are usually dwarfed by labor, real estate, transportation, energy, and tax considerations in relocation decisions, according to surveys of corporate executives. One caveat, though. Sudden changes in pollution rules can sometimes close down individual factories and destroy jobs. Retrofitting old factories can be extremely expensive, and small or marginal businesses cannot always survive government demands to make changes.

Empirical evidence confirms that the rigor of state environmental policies generally has little influence on business location. Economists, who have found the issue hard to analyze because of the paucity of information about business relocation and the complexity of environmental policy, have generally found no strong association between environmental compliance costs and business location. Studies during the Reagan administration, when national oversight lessened, found no evidence of businesses moving in search of pollution havens. Likewise, there is little evidence that international businesses seek pollution havens, according to a recent report by the Organization for Economic Cooperation and Development.

At times, businesses may choose a high standard of environmental protection for reasons having nothing to do with state law. Investors stung by plummeting Rust Belt stock prices in the 1970s, when companies predicted devastating costs to comply with the first wave of environmental laws, now want to know that firms have planned for new requirements. And firms with plants in many locations may find it economical to adhere to a single set of environmental standards.

States Have Changed

States in the 1990s bear little resemblance to states in the 1960s, and their role in environmental protection has fundamentally changed.

As political entities, they have been transformed by growth of professional staffs, vigorous two-party systems, use of referenda and initiatives to make policy, and procedural requirements that assure greater public participation in regulatory decisions.

Many aspects of environmental protection have been assimilated into state and local politics, as they have been into national politics. Political scientist Barry Rabe notes in Environmental Protection in the 1990s that about 70 percent of important environmental legislation enacted by the states now has little or nothing to do with national policy and only about 20 percent of the $10 billion that states now spend annually on environment and natural resources comes from Washington. State and local governments are responsible for nearly all the enforcement of national environmental laws and continue to dominate decisions in areas like land use and waste disposal. Occasionally, states have cooperated to spread the costs of addressing a complex problem or to concentrate pressures for action among affected states. Lax enforcement still occurs, of course, but it is more likely to be checked by political interests within the state.

Public Attitudes Have Changed

Finally, the idea that states routinely minimize environmental protection to attract business is outdated because we have learned a few things in the past 25 years about the benefits—and costs—of environmental protection. Even without a federal prod, voters have shown that they are sometimes willing to pay for state or local clean-up or conservation if they can reap the rewards. Environmental measures that contribute to critical infrastructure, attract skilled workers, or satisfy the needs of particular businesses are rightly seen as having economic value. Governors and legislators support environmental proposals that promote safe drinking water or provide adequate sanitation not because Washington requires it but because public health is a precondition to prosperity. Voters approve measures that improve an area's appeal as a place to live and work in part because catering to the preferences of skilled workers can enhance economic growth. And tourism (accounting for nearly 10 percent of US jobs in 1995) is not the only business with a direct interest in pollution control or conservation. Firms that require large amounts of pure water, for example—computer-chip manufacturers, food-processing companies, and breweries, to name a few—have economic incentives to keep streams, rivers, and groundwater uncontaminated.

At the other extreme, spending money to clean up pollution that drifts, flows, seeps, or can be transported into other states is likely to be viewed as a poor prospect by state politicians. And giving up prime development land to protect endangered species is usually seen as offering scant economic or political benefits. Environmental scientists must consider effects of development on future generations. State politicians usually can't. When poor investments for states are priorities for the nation, rigorous federal oversight is needed.

A Race to the Bottom Line

In general, though, support for environmental protection is a result, not a cause, of prosperity. At least at the extremes, states with strong economies tend to support relatively strong environmental protection programs while those with weak economies often support weaker programs.

In the 1990s, the real competition among states is not a race to the bottom to minimize environmental protection, but a race to the bottom line to improve property values and increase tax revenues. States compete to gain prosperity in an economy where firms are consolidating, capital is increasingly mobile, and skilled workers are sometimes in short supply.

Because experience has shown that wealthy economies devote more resources to environmental protection than do struggling ones, we should be concerned about the future of pollution control and conservation in relatively poor states.

Some research has suggested direct links between prosperity and environmental protection. An analysis by the Institute for

Southern Studies in 1994 found that 9 of the 12 states that were strongest in environmental protection also were strongest in economic growth, while 12 of the 14 states that were weakest in environmental protection also ranked among the lowest in economic growth. States that have been dependent on oil, timber, mining, or other natural resource industries may face special problems with improving environmental protection and with assembling the ingredients of lasting growth.

Such differences among states are not surprising. State boundaries were drawn by accidents of settlement and political compromise, not by a desire for equity. Those chance divisions have produced variations in political culture and history that, in general, we celebrate. They have also produced variations in natural resources and taxable assets. State environmental protection, which lies at a junction of economic forces, political will, and historical tradition, naturally reflects such enduring differences.

One danger, though, is that states that are weak in both economic growth and environmental protection are particularly vulnerable to a funding squeeze that may turn out to be an important political dynamic during the next 10 years—the prospect of increasing demands for environmental protection that no one is willing or able to pay for. Many of the least prosperous states depend most heavily on federal funds to finance environmental protection at a time when such funds are increasingly scarce. And their budgets are likely to be more heavily burdened by demands like welfare and Medicaid and less easily expandable by tax increases or borrowing.

None of this is an argument for economic determinism, however. State economies are constantly changing as markets change, and experience has shown that political will and fortuitous circumstances can overcome obstacles to growth. Booming high-tech industries and tourism made the Rocky Mountain states, traditionally dependent on mining, timber, and agriculture, the fastest-growing region of the country in the early 1990s. And the recent opening of the $11 million Jack Nicklaus-designed Old

Works Golf Course in Anaconda, Montana, built atop a Superfund site, is not an isolated event.

What to Do?

Giving up on the simplistic theme of a race to the bottom among states to minimize environmental protection opens the way for considering harder questions. How much flexibility should states have to make choices about environmental measures? How can national priorities not in the interest of any one state best be advanced? How should chronic inequities among states be dealt with? A number of initiatives already under way suggest partial answers.

Variations on National Themes

Setting clear national goals and giving states as much flexibility as possible in how to carry them out is the best way to mediate between national priorities and state differences. Supplementing standards with wider use of market incentives, negotiated solutions, and business self-monitoring can broaden local choices while respecting national priorities. The federal government should concentrate oversight wherever states are weakest, as the National Academy of Public Administration has suggested. And as information improves, state progress should be judged by environmental conditions, not by numbers of inspections and permits. All this is, of course, much easier said than done. After 30 years of efforts and billions of dollars spent, the United States does not yet have a reliable system of measuring trends in environmental conditions that could be a basis for setting national goals and marking progress toward them.

Information as Regulation

Requiring that the public receive detailed information about environmental consequences can create incentives for business and governments to limit pollution, particularly if the consequences directly affect those receiving the information and if facts are accompanied by objective interpretation. Using "Surf Your

Watershed," the newest EPA Internet site, for example, anyone who enters a zip code can now learn about pollution sources, water quality, and drinking water sources. And the 1996 Amendments to the Safe Drinking Water Act, passed by the 104th Congress after two years of acrimony, require local water systems to notify customers once a year about bacteria and chemicals in tap water as one way of encouraging careful monitoring. These information requirements follow the example of the Toxic Release Inventory, a provision added to federal law in 1986 and recently expanded, which requires companies to report on their discharges of toxic substances. Regional cooperation. The possible benefits of regional cooperation have received too little attention in a political system that emphasizes national and state authority. Many environmental problems are inherently regional in scope, rather than national or local. We need to understand better why some attempts at regional cooperation succeed and others fail.

Creative Financing

Voters who have effectively capped state revenues by resisting tax increases remain willing to pay special fees for environmental services or projects that are viewed as needed investments, helping to alleviate the funding squeeze, especially for the least prosperous states. Three-quarters of state and local waste disposal programs are financed by special fees, a proportion that has increased rapidly in the 1990s, according to a 1995 General Accounting Office report. Special fees also have disadvantages, of course. Linking revenue-raising to spending on particular activities can interfere with the agility of the political system in responding to changing public needs.

Changing Times

It would be a mistake to let the fears of the 1970s dominate action in the 2000s. The race to the bottom is a powerful idea that resonated with sudden changes in environmental requirements during the 1970s. It has little bearing on the challenges of the

1990s, when environmental costs are a relatively small portion of business expenses, state governments are more open to include environmental interests, and public understanding has improved. After nearly 30 years, environmental protection has been assimilated into the political system, where it will continue to evolve in thousands of separate national, state, local, and private actions. The success of those actions depends in part on our ability to adapt our ideas about how governments and businesses work to changing circumstances. In a time of scarce national resources and continuing disparities among states that are successful in economic growth and environmental protection and those that are less successful at both, our attention should now turn from the race to the bottom to the race to the bottom line.

Offshoring Causes Environmental Threats to Hosting Countries

Jai-Young Choi and Eden S. H. Yu

Jai-Young Choi is a professor of economics at Lamar University in Texas, and Eden S. H. Yu is a professor of economics and Former dean of arts and sciences at the City University of Hong Kong.

In recent decades, amid the increasing trend of globalization, it has become prevalent in world trade that firms in some countries outsource intermediate and/or finished goods or services from other firms in foreign countries for the purpose of lowering production costs and increasing production efficiency. For example, client firms in developed countries in the North (i.e., the United States [US] and the European Union [EU]), while maintaining their management bases and conducting research and development at home, shift their manufacturing activities to developing countries in the South, where labor costs are lower (e.g., the People's Republic of China [PRC], India, Malaysia, Philippines, Thailand, and Viet Nam), and/or buy a substantial amount of parts or services from local firms there.

It is noteworthy that while the focus of attention on international outsourcing (also known as "offshoring" or "fragmentation") has been largely placed on North-South outsourcing, a firm's decision to outsource can actually be driven by a variety of factors, including, but not limited to, lower labor costs. These factors can include capital, technology, and organizational competency aiming to enhance the operational capability and profitability of the firm's production. To illustrate, the US and EU countries outsource products from each other. The PRC outsources a variety of intermediate goods (such as crude petroleum, integrated circuits, and iron ore) from

"International outsourcing, environmental costs, and welfare," by Jai-Young Choi and Eden S. H. Yu, Asia Development Bank Institute, December 6, 2017, https://www.asiapathways-adbi.org/2017/12/international-outsourcing-environmental-costs-and-welfare/. This article was first published in Asia Pathways, the blog of the Asian Development Bank Institute (www.asiapathways-adbi.org). Licensed under CC BY-SA 3.0.

Australia; Germany; Hong Kong, China; Japan; and the Republic of Korea, among others, while itself shifting the outsourcing of goods (garments, apparel, toys, footwear, and tools) to other developing countries in Asia, Latin America, and Africa. The evolution of these outsourcing patterns in recent years reveals several important facts. First, outsourcing can occur universally among countries, whereby it can be in any direction. Second, each time goods and services are imported, the importing country may have outsourced a portion of economic activity from abroad—that is, all trade is likely to involve some outsourcing of intermediate inputs. Third, for trading countries and the world, free trade with outsourcing is always superior, or at least equivalent, to free trade without outsourcing because outsourcing is a state of free trade coupled with partial factor migration among nations.

Meanwhile, in the international outsourcing frontier, a notable development has been occurring for the South. Namely, following the PRC's accession to the World Trade Organization in 2001, the dramatic expansion of North-South trade and outsourcing by Northern firms to the South has inflicted massive damage on the once clean air and fertile soil in the South. A marked example is the case of the PRC as the so-called "world factory," where the production of myriad outsourced goods and services (i.e., garments, apparel, toys, footwear, tools, light machinery, electronics, and information technology products) is contaminating air, water, and soil, and depleting labor and material pools, triggering deforestation, desertification and global warming, and seriously endangering public health. However, the vendor countries in the South are mostly developing countries with the primary goal of economic development. Hence, despite the environmental damage, they opt in their early period of international offshoring to provide a hospitable business environment to the Northern outsourcing firms.

But, as outsourcing activities expand, the environmental costs resulting from the outsourcing became too heavy for the vendor countries to bear. Therefore, beginning from about a decade and half ago, the major vendor countries (notably the PRC) have begun to account for or internalize the environmental costs of outsourcing by enacting environmental regulations and taxes. This policy shift increases the prices of their outsourced goods and services for the firms in the North. However, the extent of such a move is considerably below the level that can bring back the South to an acceptable environmental quality specified by World Health Organization standards. This argument is supported by numerous observations reported on the presently stagnating or regionally deteriorating environmental quality in the PRC and its neighboring countries, including the Republic of Korea, Cambodia, India, the Lao People's Democratic Republic, Malaysia, and the Philippines. To quote a few from the recent reports by mass media:

> "The cost of environmental degradation in [the PRC] was about $230 billion in 2010, or 3.5 percent of the nation's gross domestic product—three times that in 2004, in local currency terms." (New York Times 2013)
>
> "The acidic deposition damages buildings, degrades the environment and reduces crop yields. In India, wheat growing near a power plant suffered a 49% reduction in yield compared with that grown 22 kilometers away." (Global Warming 2009)

Another development in international outsourcing is that many Northern firms have adopted new strategies to counter the rising costs of outsourcing brought by Southern regulations. They have resorted to vendor-country diversification, partial outsourcing, insourcing, or resourcing. Since the mid-2000s, there have been numerous reports about the changing patterns of outsourcing by Northern firms.

The theory of distortions in international trade stipulates that free trade is the optimal policy for a nation and the world with no distortions, but, in a world of second-best with distortion, policy intervention may be better for a nation than doing nothing. On policy intervention in the presence of distortion, the Specificity Rule prescribes that the policy should directly target the cause of the problem. The policy implication of the Specificity Rule is clear: to fully resolve the environmental problem in the South, strengthening regulation or fostering international cooperation is desirable for implementation until the environmental costs of outsourcing are fully accounted for by the outsourcing firms in the North.

Industrialization Affects Air Quality in India and China

K. S. Venkatachalam

K. S. Venkatachalam is a freelance columnist and political commentator who writes for the Diplomat.

The Health Effects Institute (HEI), a Boston-based non-profit organization that specializes in studying health effects as a result of pollution, recently published its "State of Global Air, 2017: A Special Report on Global Exposure to Air Pollution and its Disease Burden." Based on extensive research conducted across 175 countries, HEI found that India and China face the deadliest air pollution in the world.

The study reveals that air pollution has caused over 4.2 million early deaths across the globe in 2015, out of which India and China alone accounted for 25.7 percent and 26.1 percent respectively. HEI focuses on two measures of outdoor air pollution in their Global Burden of Disease Project: ambient fine particulate matter (airborne particles less than or equal to 2.5 micrometers in diameter, or PM2.5) and ozone, a reactive gas. These are the most widely studied and monitored air pollutants worldwide, with PM2.5 responsible for the vast majority of early deaths (4.2 million, compared to 254,000 attributed to ozone).

In India, rapid industrialization and population growth have adversely affected urban climates, particularly air quality, and caused imbalances in the regional climate at large. As per a study conducted by the World Health Organization, half of world's 20 most polluted cities are in India.

There are several reasons for the alarming increase in air pollution. The total vehicles sold in India have increased by over 273 percent since 2000. The exposure to vehicle exhaust has led to a significant increase in respiratory symptoms, cancer, and lung function impairments. Unfortunately, India has yet to come out with a definite roadmap for setting emission standards throughout the country.

India and Bangladesh have experienced the steepest increases in pollution since 2010, and now have the highest PM2.5 concentrations in the world. In India, the air pollution has gone beyond safe exposure levels and, in some of Indian cities, has led to a steep increase in premature deaths.

China has recorded the highest number of deaths as a result of pollution, but by declaring air pollution a national disaster they have taken several steps to control the damage. China has thus been able to reduce the death rate by 2 percent. However, in India, over the same period, deaths have gone up by 1.4 percent. Globally, there was a 60 percent increase in ozone-attributable deaths, with a striking 67 percent of this increase occurring in India. Ozone-related deaths have gone up by 148 percent in India, while China saw an increase of only 0.41 percent.

It is here that India can learn from the Chinese experience. Recently, many big cities in China were faced with the problem of choking smog. In Beijing, the concentration of fine particulate matter reached 40 times the exposure limit recommended by the WHO. China has taken some strong measure since then to control air pollution. As China burns half of the coal consumed in the world, it has now set limits on the burning of coal and is transitioning to lower emission coal burning technologies. The dust concentration by the coal-burning boilers in thermal power plants has been reduced from 30 milligrams per cubic meter to 20 milligrams per cubic meter. China has also taken high-polluting vehicles, those registered before the end of 2005, off the roads. In a significant step, Beijing has also directed steel and cement manufacturing units to cut down on their production—a move driven primarily by a global surplus in those materials, but with the beneficial side effect of a drop in the concentration of particulate matter in cities.

China has also taken measures to restrict traffic flow during periods of heavy pollution. This, coupled with cloud seeding for clearing the smog, especially in Beijing, has had an impact. The State Council has directed officials to treat heavy pollution as a natural disaster and has directed local governments to enact emergency management response measures during periods of heavy pollution. The State Council has also been directed not to grant loans to industries that have not passed the environmental assessment system. Those projects that do not get the mandated clearances would not be provided with electricity and water.

The challenge before India, as compared to China, is more complex, as it is still in the nascent stage of industrialization. It will be a real challenge to emulate China, which is facing the problem of excess capacity in the steel and cement industries. Moreover, like China, India depends on cheap coal for power generation, and it is years away from switching completely to renewable energy.

India, however, can learn from the Chinese experience of installing basic pollution abatement equipment in almost all its thermal power plants. India has installed such equipment in only 10 percent of its power plants. China, by switching to high-efficiency, low-emissions (HELE) coal technologies, has also made its coal-fired power plants more efficient. India can also draw from the Chinese experience of restricting traffic flow and using cloud seeding, especially in the national capital, during periods of heavy smog. It also needs to establish a proper waste disposal system, as we have lately seen fires breaking out in waste-dumping sites in Mumbai and Bangalore. Further, in view of the Indian Supreme Court's decision to ban registration of luxury SUVs and diesel cars above 2000 cc in the national capital, immediate steps need to be taken to improve the public transport system in all major cities.

The Indian government needs to come out with a comprehensive plan for addressing the issue of air pollution. If proper steps are taken, India, like China, will succeed in controlling air pollution by keeping the Air Quality Index below 100, which falls under the moderate level of health concerns. These steps will help India to realize its environmental and social responsibilities.

Air Pollution from Industrial Practices Is Also Prevalent in the United States

Nate Berg

Nate Berg is a journalist who writes about cities, design, and technology. His work has previously appeared in the New York Times, Wired, *and* Architect.

The bluffs on Panorama Road offer a wide view of the northern half of Bakersfield, which is one of the few major population centres in California's Central Valley—perhaps the US' leading agricultural motherlode.

It's a rare bird's eye vantage point of this low-slung farm city of roughly 375,000 people, nestled in a bowl created by the Sierra Nevada mountains to the east and part of the California Coast Ranges to the west. On a clear day, the state's dominant topographical features put the landscape, and one's place in it, in sobering perspective.

But clear days don't happen all that often in Bakersfield. Emissions from agriculture, industry, rail freight and road traffic together create one of the country's worst concentrations of air pollution—a condition exacerbated by geographic and climatic conditions that trap dry, dirty air over this southern section of Central Valley like the lid over a pot.

Oil fields make up most of the view from the top of the bluffs, and the scent of petroleum is often detectable around the city. Dairies populated by hundreds of thousands of cows are scattered throughout the region, and their smell, too, is hard to miss. Massive warehouses and distribution centres on the outskirts of town bring in diesel trucks day and night from Interstate 5, the major north-south route that runs from Canada to Mexico (Los Angeles is

"Breathless in Bakersfield: is the worst air pollution in the US about to get worse?" by Nate Berg, Guardian News and Media Limited, February 14, 2017. Reprinted by permission.

about 100 miles to the south). Freight trains hauling oil rumble through the city, and its many refineries billow smoke into the air.

Bakersfield and surrounding Kern County are the unlucky nexus of this pollution. The American Lung Association's State of the Air 2016 report found the city's air to be the worst in the United States for short-term and year-round particle pollution, and the second worst for ozone pollution.

One of the main indicators of poor air quality is the level of fine particulate matter (PM2.5) in the air. The WHO's latest ambient air pollution database ranks nearby Visalia-Porterville worst in the US. Bakersfield's average reading in one 24-hour period in late January was 40.5 micrograms per cubic metre; over the mountains in somewhat smoggy Los Angeles, that number averages about 12.

Of the wider metro area's 875,000 people, about 70,000 are said to have asthma, 40,000 cardiovascular disease, and 27,000 chronic obstructive pulmonary disease. A 2006 study found the health impacts of the region's air pollution cost the southern section of the Central Valley, known as the San Joaquin, an estimated $3bn (£2.4bn)—or about $1,000 per person per year in a region where about a quarter of the population is in poverty.

Though some improvements have been made in recent years through more stringent air quality standards, cleaner burning engines and efficient industrial machinery, the region continues to struggle with poor air quality and the health problems it brings. Now the election of Donald Trump to the presidency, and his appointment of an Environmental Protection Agency (EPA) head in Scott Pruitt who is actively opposed air quality regulations, has many worried that the small but steady improvements to the area's air quality may all be undone.

Gustavo Aguirre Jr is a prominent local activist who works on environmental justice issues in many of the small, underserved and impoverished farming communities that surround Bakersfield. He says progress has been slow in the San Joaquin Valley, a conservative part of the state that's heavily influenced by agricultural and oil industry interests, and the Trump administration could further limit that progress.

"The potential of us going backwards 50 or 60 years in air pollution control and mitigation is very scary," says Aguirre. The worst air in the United States may soon be getting worse.

But the authority tasked with addressing the region's air quality issues, the San Joaquin Valley Air Pollution Control District, does not seem too concerned, suggesting it has done just about all it can to alleviate the problem.

"Over the last 25 years, air pollution in the San Joaquin Valley—from the stationary sources we regulate—has been reduced by over 80% with some of the toughest air regulations in place anywhere in the nation," says Seyed Sadredin, the air district's executive director.

These improvements have come through working with farmers to reduce the burning of agricultural waste, funding trade-ins for older farm equipment, and imposing requirements for cleaner burning furnaces and fireplaces, among other measures. Now, Sadredin argues, it is up to the state of California's Air Resources Board to better regulate mobile pollution sources—the cars, diesel trucks and freight trains—that are under the state's purview.

"The biggest pollution source right now that's holding us back is the nitrogen oxide emissions from the mobile sources that make up 85% of the pollution," he adds.

Indeed, Sadredin has begun calling for revisions to the Clean Air Act, a landmark federal law overseeing environmental standards in the US, as a way to reduce or even eliminate the estimated $30m a year in sanctions and fines that have been placed on the valley because of its failure to meet federal clean air standards.

A November 2016 air district white paper directed to the presidential transition team makes the argument that the valley is unfairly punished by the existing provisions of the Clean Air Act, and calls for changes.

"We should have a more receptive ear at the EPA, if you read the tea leaves in the coming administration, that would pay attention to the economic devastation that some of these sanctions could cause to poor regions like ours," Sadredin says.

He'd prefer to make these changes through new legislation, like the air pollution bill passed by the House of Representatives last year but was stalled before the end of the legislative session. "[But] given the political dynamics and the divisiveness in Washington, getting a clean piece of legislation like that may be difficult, so we may ultimately be in a position that I hope we don't have to be in, where we have to attach what we need to something that perhaps does more than people like to see by way of changes to the Clean Air Act," Sadredin warns.

Environmentalists and activists in Kern County worry that such a heavy-handed approach will erode the Clean Air Act, reducing regulations on Bakersfield's highly polluting industries.

"It takes away the need to meet the standard no matter what it costs, because [Sadredin] wants language in there that reduces responsibility if it's economically or technologically unfeasible," says Tom Frantz, a local almond farmer and outspoken environmental activist. "And once you get language like that into the Clean Air Act, you can justify not doing almost anything for technological or economic reasons. You have this huge loophole.

"The San Joaquin Valley air pollution control district has claimed repeatedly that they've done all they should be expected to do," Frantz adds. "They have every excuse in the world of why they've done enough. So our real enemy in this, from my side of things, is our own air district—which refuses to recognise the health costs of our continuing pollution levels, and is unwilling to do whatever's necessary to get it cleaned up."

"We Have to Fight"

While the results of the 2016 elections haven't been welcomed by all in Bakersfield, last year was a good one for the area's air quality. For the first time in nearly 20 years, the valley avoided violation of state and federal regulations for the concentration of PM2.5s: particulate matter that's 2.5 micrometers in diameter or smaller (roughly a 20th of the width of a human hair). These particles are a key measure of air quality because they're too small to be stopped from lodging in the lungs, and contribute to a variety of pulmonary and cardiovascular diseases.

After six years of extreme drought, a series of storms last year is credited with moving enough of the valley's air to bring down the PM2.5 measurements. "The valley we live in has stagnant high-pressure systems that will sit for up to a month, even six weeks," Frantz says. "Any time a low-pressure system comes off the Pacific, it blows out our bad air. If that would happen once a week, we would not have much of an air quality problem."

What also helped, he says, is the drop in prices for both oil and milk, two market conditions that resulted in reduced output from the region's refineries and dairies, and thus fewer of their polluting emissions. "When they pull back a little bit because of low prices, we get a little bit cleaner air," Frantz says.

But, he notes, those dairies and refineries could soon be operating at greater capacity again—and while the region got lucky with rain last year, normal annual rainfall in Bakersfield is just 6.47 inches. Without stronger environmental regulations, he warns, Bakersfield could be stuck with its worst-ranked air quality for a long time to come.

Some aren't waiting for action at the federal level. In the front room of a Boys and Girls Club in the tiny farmworker community of Lamont, just south of Bakersfield, around 25 community activists from a handful of local organisations have gathered to coordinate their efforts around environmental justice issues in Kern County. Planners at the county are currently working on a new countywide general plan, and recent legislationrequires them to take into consideration environmental justice issues.

Aguirre says the groups have to be strategic about how and where they advance their agenda. "We've made some progress at statewide level with the governor of California—but locally our pollution control district is an ultraconservative, pro-industry air district that says yes to everything from industry and no to the community."

To push back, he's working with a nearby community called Arvin to install a set of air pollution monitors throughout this small city to track PM2.5, ozone and other harmful pollutants. Aguirre is hoping to collect data to show local officials that air pollution issues here are much worse than the state and air district monitors report.

He says small communities, especially those most affected by the region's poor air quality and other environmental issues, have to become more involved in documenting the conditions that pose public health risks. If they don't, he argues, nobody else will.

"We have to fight," Aguirre says. "Tooth and nail."

A Greener Future

Compared to years past, Bakersfield's air has improved significantly, according to Bob Smith, a local real estate developer and Bakersfield city council member. "I think it's a success story in a lot of ways," he says.

Smith argues that state and local regulations have played a large role in reducing air pollution in the city and the valley, as have industrial investments in cleaner technologies. Various state grants and incentive programmes have also helped reduce pollution, offering trade-ins or tune-ups for older vehicles and incentivising the adoption of cleaner burning farm equipment.

Now Smith sees the potential for even more improvements. A bicycle advocate who rides through downtown Bakersfield on a new electric Dutch-style cargo bike, Smith has been trying to make the case that alternative forms of transportation can help reduce the city's air pollution. He helped establish the city's first bicycle transportation plan in 2013, and also pushed the city to adopt a resolution in support of a Complete Streets policy that refocuses road planning to accommodate pedestrians, cyclists and other forms of transportation in addition to cars.

Walking down 18th street, a mostly sleepy commercial corridor in downtown Bakersfield, Smith points out a cafe he's helping to develop, and a 44-unit market-rate apartment project he's building a block away. They are two bets on the future of downtown, but also on the future of a more cosmopolitan style of city—not a traditional farm town renowned for its trucks and cowboy hats.

But while Smith is optimistic about a greener future for the city, he also notes that its population grew by more than 100,000 people from 2000 to 2010—one of the fastest rates of growth in the country. As more people move to the region, addressing pollution from vehicles and homes becomes even more important. Getting more people on bikes, or at least out of cars, will surely only help.

The United States Saw a Record-Breaking Spike in Crude Oil Production in 2018

US Energy Information Administration

The US Energy Information Administration provides information on energy production and use as well as how it interacts with the economy and the environment to help government officials make appropriate energy-related decisions.

The United States uses and produces many different types and sources of energy, which can be grouped into general categories such as primary and secondary, renewable and nonrenewable, and fossil fuels.

Primary energy sources include fossil fuels (petroleum, natural gas, and coal), nuclear energy, and renewable sources of energy. Electricity is a secondary energy source that is generated (produced) from primary energy sources.

Energy sources are measured in different physical units: liquid fuels in barrels or gallons, natural gas in cubic feet, coal in short tons, and electricity in kilowatts and kilowatthours. In the United States, British thermal units (Btu), a measure of heat energy, is commonly used for comparing different types of energy to each other. In 2018, total US primary energy consumption was equal to about 101,251,057,000,000,000 British thermal units (Btu), or about 101.3 quadrillion Btu.

In 2018, the electric power sector accounted for about 96% of total US electricity generation, nearly all of which was sold to the other sectors.[1]

The transportation, industrial, commercial, and residential sectors are called *end-use sectors* because they consume primary energy and electricity produced by the electric power sector.

"The United States uses a mix of energy sources," US Energy Information Administration, August 28, 2019. Reprinted by permission.

The sources of energy used by each sector varies widely. For example, petroleum provides about 92% of the transportation sector's energy consumption, but less than 1% of the electric power sector's primary energy use. The chart below shows the types and amounts of primary energy sources consumed in the United States, the amounts of primary energy used by the electric power sector and the energy end-use sectors, and the sales of retail electricity by the electric power sector to the energy end-use sectors.

Total energy consumption by the end-use sectors includes their primary energy use, purchased electricity, and electrical system energy losses (energy conversion and other losses associated with the generation, transmission, and distribution of purchased electricity) and other energy losses.

Domestic Energy Production Equaled About 95% of US Energy Consumption in 2018

In 2018, the amount of energy produced in the United States was equal to about 95.7 quads, which was equal to about 95% of total US energy consumption, the largest share since 1967. Net imports of crude oil accounted for the majority of the difference between total primary energy production and total primary energy consumption in 2018.

Fossil fuels—petroleum, natural gas, and coal—accounted for about 79% of total US primary energy production in 2018.

The Mix of US Energy Consumption and Production Has Changed Over Time

Fossil fuels have dominated the US energy mix for more than 100 years, but the mix has changed over time.

Coal production has trended down since its peak of 24.0 quads in 1998. A major reason for the general decline in US coal production in recent years is the decrease in US coal consumption for electricity generation.

Natural gas production reached a record high of 31.5 quads in 2018. In 2017 and 2018, US dry natural gas production was greater than US natural gas consumption for the first time since 1966. More efficient drilling and production techniques have resulted in increased production of natural gas from shale and tight geologic formations. The increase in production contributed to a decline in natural gas prices, which in turn has contributed to increases in natural gas use by the electric power and industrial sectors.

Crude oil production generally decreased each year between 1970 and 2008. In 2009, the trend reversed and production began to rise, and in 2018, US crude oil production was 22.8 quads, the highest on record. More cost-effective drilling and production technologies helped to boost production, especially in Texas and North Dakota.

Natural gas plant liquids (NGPL) are hydrocarbon gas liquids (HGL) that are extracted from natural gas before the natural gas is put into pipelines for transmission to consumers. NGPL production has increased alongside increases in natural gas production and reached a record high of 5.8 quads in 2018. US HGL consumption and exports to other countries have both increased in recent years.

Nuclear energy production in commercial nuclear power plants in the United States began in 1957 and grew each year through 1990 and generally leveled off after 2000. In 2018, even though there were fewer operating nuclear reactors than in 2000, nuclear power plants produced the second-highest amount of energy on record at 8.4 quads, mainly because of a combination of increased capacity from power plant upgrades and shorter refueling and maintenance cycles.

Renewable energy production and consumption both reached record highs of about 11.7 and 11.5 quads, respectively, in 2018. Although hydroelectric power production in 2018 was about 6% lower than the 50-year average, biomass, wind, solar, and geothermal energy production were higher than in any previous year.

Notes

1. The industrial, commercial, and residential sectors produced about 4% of total electricity generation in 2018. A small amount of electricity is imported from and exported to Canada and Mexico.

Organizations to Contact

The editors have compiled the following list of organizations concerned with the issues debated in this book. The descriptions are derived from materials provided by the organizations. All have publications or information available for interested readers. This list was compiled on the date of publication of the present volume; the information provided here may change. Be aware that many organizations take several weeks or longer to respond to inquiries, so allow as much time as possible.

Alliance for American Manufacturing (AAM)
711 D Street NW
3rd Floor
Washington, DC 20004
phone: (202) 393-3430
email: info@aamfg.org
website: www.americanmanufacturing.org

The Alliance for American Manufacturing (AAM) was founded by some of the top manufacturers in the United States to promote keeping jobs in the country and to focus on making a positive impact in the economy. The alliance works on building important public policies to answer to the needs of manufacturing workers and the industrial sector.

Association for Advancing Automation (A3)
900 Victors Way
Suite 140
Ann Arbor, MI 48108
phone: (734) 994-6088
email: info@a3automate.org
website: www.a3automate.org

The Association for Advancing Automation is the umbrella organization for Robotic Industries Association, the Motion Control and Motor Association, and other automation organizations and manufacturers. It works to advocate for the benefits of automating. A3 hosts trade shows and conferences and provides its members with market research to help them achieve their goals.

The Association for Manufacturing Technology (AMT)

7901 Jones Branch Drive
Suite 900
McLean, VA 22102-3316
phone: (703) 893-2900
email: AMT@AMTonline.org
website: www.amtonline.org

The Association for Manufacturing Technology champions US-based manufacturing technology. Its members are responsible for building, designing, and selling the technologies essential to the manufacturing business. It also annually hosts the International Manufacturing Technology Show.

Center for Climate and Energy Solutions

3100 Clarendon Boulevard
Suite 800
Arlington, VA 22201
phone: (703) 516-4146
email: press@C2ES.org
website: www.c2es.org

Promoting clean energy, strengthening resilience to climate impacts, and reducing greenhouse gas emissions are the three goals of the Center for Climate and Energy Solutions. Its mission is to promote efficient policymaking to help in the fight against climate change. This prominent organization succeeds the Pew Center on Global Climate Change, which was founded in 1998.

Citizens' Climate Lobby

1330 Orange Avenue

#309

Coronado, CA 92118

phone: (619) 437-7142

website: www.citizensclimatelobby.org

The Citizens' Climate Lobby is a nonpartisan advocacy organization focused on bringing awareness to climate change. They train volunteers to build a more effective relationship with their local elected officials to push sustainable actions to fight climate change. As part of their efforts, they support the Energy Innovation and Carbon Dividend Act, which was introduced on January 24, 2019.

Climate Action Network (CAN)

Kaiserstr. 201

Bonn, 53113

Germany

email: administration@climatenetwork.org

website: www.climatenetwork.org

The Climate Action Network is comprised of 1,300 independent non-governmental organizations based in approximately 120 countries. The network advocates for governmental and individual initiatives that can help curb the climate crisis. Additionally, the network helps CAN members exchange information on how they can each tackle climate issues.

The Climate Reality Project

555 11th Street NW

Suite 601

Washington, DC 20004

website: www.climaterealityproject.org

The Climate Reality Project was founded by former US vice president Al Gore. After releasing the documentary *An Inconvenient Truth*, he moved to take action toward reversing climate change with a project that unifies people around the world. It now has more than 20,000 Climate Reality leaders in approximately 150 countries.

Fair Labor Association
2033 K Street NW
Suite 400
Washington, DC 20006
phone: (202) 898-1000
email: info@fairlabor.org
website: www.fairlabor.org

Founded in 1999, the mission of the Fair Labor Association is to improve the lives of workers globally. The association is made of universities, colleges, civil society organizations, and socially responsible companies. The group focuses on making sure that labor conditions in factories around the world are acceptable.

Greenpeace
702 H Street NW
Suite 300
Washington, DC 20001
phone: (202) 462-1177
email: info@wdc.greenpeace.org
website: www.greenpeace.org

Greenpeace is an organization that campaigns for more sustainable actions to curb climate change. It was founded in 1971.

The International Society of Automation (ISA)
67 T. W. Alexander Drive
PO Box 12277
Research Triangle Park, NC 27709
phone: (919) 549-8411
email: info@isa.org
website: www.isa.org

Founded in 1945, the International Society of Automation is a nonprofit organization connecting automation professionals.

It publishes books and technical articles, certifies industry professionals, and trains members. This organization is comprised of 40,000 members and 400,000 customers.

Manufacturing Solutions Center
301 Conover Station SE
Conover, NC 28613
phone: (828) 327-7000 ext. 4265
email: lyork@manufacturingsolutionscenter.org
website: www.manufacturingsolutionscenter.org

The mission of the Manufacturing Solutions Center is simple: find ways to help US manufactures increase sales, improve quality, and improve efficiency to create or retain jobs. To do so, the center focuses on ten specific initiatives, including enhancing and improving products through research and development, training personnel for lean manufacturing processes and supply chain efficiencies, and providing hands-on guidance for international marketing, sales, and military procurement. The center is an initiative by the Catawba Valley Community College.

National Association of Manufacturers (NAM)
733 10th Street NW
Suite 700
Washington, DC 20001
phone: (202) 637-3000
email: manufacturing@nam.org
website: www.nam.org

This association has 1,400 member companies in the industrial sector. It serves as both a resource and advocacy center for manufacturers. The organization focuses on promoting sustainability, fostering new research, and advocating for innovative labor policies.

National Day Laborer Organizing Network (NDLON)
1030 S. Arroyo Parkway
Suite 106
Pasadena, CA 91105
phone: (626) 799-3566
website: www.ndlon.org

The National Day Laborer Organizing Network was founded in 2001. Its goal is to improve the lives of day laborers, migrants, and low-wage workers. The network started with twelve community-based organizations, but grew to become a national network. It aims to achieve its goal of social change through nonviolent resistance.

United Students Against Sweatshops (USAS)
1155 Connecticut Avenue NW
Suite 500
Washington, DC 20036
website: www.usas.org

This labor-campaign organization has more than 150 chapters in campuses around the country. It is a student-led organization that was founded in 1997 to bring economic justice to domestic workers and workers abroad. It particularly focuses on protecting university workers and those who work overseas to make collegiate apparel.

Bibliography

Books

Maya Ajmera. *Every Breath We Take: A Book About Air.* Watertown, MA: Charlesbridge, 2016.

Sven Beckert. *Empire of Cotton: A New History Of Global Capitalism.* New York, NY: Allen Lane, 2014.

Ian Bremmer. *Us Vs. Them: The Failure of Globalism.* New York, NY: Penguin, 2018.

Adila Cokar. *Source My Garment: The Insider's Guide to Responsible Offshore Manufacturing.* Toronto, ON: Source My Garment Consulting Inc., 2019.

Joshua Benjamin Freeman. *Behemoth: A History of The Factory and The Making of The Modern World.* New York, NY: W. W. Norton & Company, 2018.

Emily Guendelsberger. *On the Clock: What Low-Wage Work Did to Me and How It Drives America Insane.* New York, NY: Little, Brown and Company, 2019.

Kari Jones. *A Fair Deal: Shopping for Social Justice.* Custer, WA: Orca Book Publishers, 2017.

Daniel Katz and Richard A. Greenwald. *Labor Rising: The Past and Future of Working People In America.* New York, NY: New Press, 2012.

Naomi Klein. *This Changes Everything: Capitalism Vs. The Climate.* New York, NY: Simon & Schuster, 2014.

Beth Macy. *Factory Man: How One Furniture Maker Battled Offshoring, Stayed Local—And Helped Save An American Town.* New York, NY: Little, Brown and Company, 2014.

David Maraniss. *Once In A Great City: A Detroit Story.* New York, NY: Simon & Schuster, 2015.

Kamal Meattle and Barun Aggarwal. *How to Grow Fresh Air*. New Delhi, India: Juggernaut Publications, 2018.

Paul Ortiz. *An African American and Latinx History of the United States*. Boston, MA: Beacon Press, 2018.

Mary Robinson. *Climate Justice: Hope, Resilience, and the Fight for A Sustainable Future*. New York, NY: Bloomsbury Publishing, 2018.

Ellen Ruppel Shell. *The Job: Work and Its Future in A Time of Radical Change*. New York, NY: Currency, 2018.

Bhu Srinivasa. *Americana: A 400-Year History of American Capitalism*. New York, NY: Penguin Press, 2017.

Adam J. Tooze. *Crashed: How A Decade of Financial Crises Changed the World*. New York, NY: Viking, 2018.

Periodicals and Internet Sources

Kopal Cheema, "India Vs. China Turns Electric: How The Two Markets Stack Up For Electric Vehicles," Inc42, December 17, 2019. https://inc42.com/features/india-vs-china-turns-electric-the-story-of-two-ev-markets/.

Glenn Daehn, "'Robotic Blacksmithing': A Technology That Could Revive US Manufacturing," SingularityHub, December 13, 2019. https://singularityhub.com/2019/12/13/robotic-blacksmithing-a-technology-that-could-revive-us-manufacturing/.

Mohamed A. El-Erian, "US-China Deal Will Be a Short-Term Truce," *Bloomberg*, December 17, 2019. https://www.bloomberg.com/opinion/articles/2019-12-17/u-s-china-trade-deal-will-be-a-short-truce-not-a-lasting-peace.

Clare Goldsberry, "How to Make US Manufacturing Great, According to Plastic Molding Manufacturing CEO," *PlasticsToday*, December 16, 2019. https://www.plasticstoday.com/injection-molding/how-make

-us-manufacturing-great-according-plastic-molding
-manufacturing-ceo/195465496962061.

Austen Hufford, "American Factories Demand White-Collar
Education for Blue-Collar Work," *Wall Street Journal*,
December 9, 2019. https://www.wsj.com/articles/american
-factories-demand-white-collar-education-for-blue-collar
-work-11575907185.

Natalie Kitroeff, "Fashion Nova's Secret: Underpaid Workers in
Los Angeles Factories," *New York Times*, December 16, 2019.
https://www.nytimes.com/2019/12/16/business/fashion-nova
-underpaid-workers.html?searchResultPosition=7.

Rachel Layne, "Boeing 737 Max Woes Could Wallop Slumping
US Manufacturing Sector," CBS News, December 17, 2019.
https://www.cbsnews.com/news/boeing-737-max-woes
-could-wallop-slumping-u-s-manufacturing-sector/.

Yen Nee Lee, "Yale's Stephen Roach Says US Manufacturers
Won't Move Out Of China So Easily," CNBC, November 25,
2019. https://www.cnbc.com/2019/11/26/stephen-roach-on
-manufacturing-supply-chain-shifts-amid-trade-war.html.

Michelle R. Matisons, "New Trade Era Will Require Pro-Labor
Policies, Green Manufacturing," MultiBriefs, December 17,
2019. http://exclusive.multibriefs.com/content/new-trade
-era-will-require-pro-labor-policies-green-manufacturing
/manufacturing.

Emma Foehringer Merchant, "Elizabeth Warren Unveils 'Blue
New Deal' With Support for Offshore Wind," Green Tech
Media, December 10, 2019. https://www.greentechmedia
.com/articles/read/warren-unveils-blue-new-deal-with
-support-for-offshore-wind

Theron Mohamed, "Trump's China Trade Deal May Be Too
Little, Too Late For Midwestern Manufacturing—And
His Reelection Chances Could Suffer," Markets Insider,
December 17, 2019. https://markets.businessinsider.com

/news/stocks/trump-china-trade-deal-late-midwestern
-manufacturing-hurts-reelection-bid-2019-12-1028768155.

Justin R. Pierce and Peter K. Schott, "The Surprisingly Swift
Decline of US Manufacturing Employment," American
Economic Association, July 2016. https://www.aeaweb.org
/articles?id=10.1257/aer.20131578.

Christopher Reynolds, "Meet the Canadian Rag Trade
Companies Holding Out Against Offshore Manufacturing,"
Star, December 9, 2019. https://www.thestar.com
/business/2019/12/08/meet-the-apparel-companies
-holding-out-against-the-offshore-manufacturing-tide
.html.

Aaron Rupar, "The Most Worrying New Survey For Trump Has
Nothing To Do With His Polling," Vox, October 2, 2019.
https://www.vox.com/2019/10/2/20893767/manufacturing
-contracting-trump-trade-war.

Murat Suner, "What Are Human Causes Of Climate Change?"
Fair Planet, December 17, 2019. https://www.fairplanet.org
/story/what-are-human-causes-of-climate-change/.

Index

5